THUNDERSQUEAK

"As well as being a particularly fine introduction to the practical side of the occult, Thundersqueak could almost be regarded as one of the ur-texts of Kaos, if not the one that set the kaos-sphere rolling." - Head Magazine, issue 5

"Thundersqueak is definitely on my list of Top Ten Most Influential Books That I Have Read" Rodney Orpheus

"This is a book to turn you on to so many things; it's hard to know where to start....
I suppose at a pinch this could be called a self-help book- as there are instructions inside that you can follow, and by doing so make your life better (or at least more interesting)- and perhaps happier- even if "the only true happiness is to live dangerously in times of peace, and to be at peace in times of crisis" ... but New-Age fluffy it is NOT! This is 'self-help by self psychic-surgery': It tears your self to bits and chucks out the crap." Kate Hoolu on www.occultebooks.com

THUNDERSQUEAK

or
the confession
of a right wing
anarchist

being
the suicide writings
of
Liz Angerford and Ambrose Lea

Edited by Ramsey Dukes
Decorations by Howard Luder

Published by The  Mouse That Spins

THUNDERSQUEAK

or

the confession of a right wing anarchist

By Liz Angerford & Ambrose Lea

First published by The Mouse That Spins December 1979
Reprint with new preface March 1989

German editions sometime in between

First e-book edition published by El-cheapo
for The Mouse That Spins 2001

First print on demand paperback reprint
by The Mouse That Spins, October 2002

ISBN: 0-904311-12-0

E-books available at web-orama.com
books@web-orama.com / publisher@el-cheapo.com

We are trained to stick up for our principles.

Not overtly: there is no school lesson and examination called "Sticking to Principles". The training is simply imbued in our culture in a deep belief that a "person of principle" is "better".

This is politically most convenient. If a government introduces some new measure, it helps the government if it can rely on all its opponents to come out onto the streets and protest. Because once they are on the streets they can be shot. Or, more realistically, once it has identified the opponents it can use that information to keep them gently out of power for ever more.

"Sticking up for your principles" is itself a priciple. It could get you shot. What sort of an ally is that?

Thundersqueak says that principles are tyrants. They are the worst tyrants of all because they dwell in your own mind.

So don't stick up for principles - fuck them.

You then discover that the principles you have been sticking up for were not "your" principles, but those most convenient to other systems.

And you begin to feel quite principled about this discovery.

No! No! NO! Not this! Not that! I will not stick up for ANY of you!

The mud was washed and now the rock is being chipped away. It is slowly revealing something very empty in its flawlessness. Something very hard in its clarity. Something utterly precious.

Through refusing to stick up for anything you have begun to stick up for your Self.

Let it go.

The real value of a diamond lies not in its substance, but in the rainbow of colours revealed to all as light passes on its way.

About this 2002 edition

I wanted to include the original illustrated initial capitals by Howard Luder - which are not in the e-book edition which has been re-typeset beautifully for screen reading. So this edition is done as a facsimile scan of the first edition.

The result is a bit crappy - but it somehow echoes the vibrations of the era that spawned Thundersqueak. So I offer this edition with fewer apologies than might be expected.

I thank those many people who expressed their appreciation of the book over the years - including Hilmar, Pete, Ian, Phil, Rodney, Joel, Arthur, Philippa, Dave... there are lots more, including a Richard who somehow made a piece of theatre around the book! Your encouragement has fuelled this reprint.

Actually - in view of the expressions of anger in the world today - it seems an appropriate time to re-read Thundersqueak. Was I the only person in the West who felt thrilled when I saw the World Trade Centre collapse? Thrilled that this symbol of our illusions of temporal power dominating the 'little man' could actually fall to the will of a handful of determined individuals?

Am I alone in understanding that this excitement does not make me a 'bad' person, but simply someone who sees meaning behind the smoke, rubble and pain?

Would I, for example, have risked my life to help rescue those among the rubble? I think I might well have done.

In that case, had I had foreknowledge of the plot, would I have tipped off the authorities and foiled it? That is a far harder question - I would have preferredto have evacuated the building just in time that three thousand more people should live to understand the power of feeling their systems had invoked.

By the way... does anyone know Howard Luder and where he is now?

Ramsey Dukes owes him one...

CONTENTS

Do you yearn to die
When the future looks bleak?
I tell you, that's the call of .... THUNDERSQUEAK

When your soul screams 'why?'
And the world won't speak –
At the back of it all lurks .... THUNDERSQUEAK

When the world seems hard, and offers no relief
From crustacean minds armoured with belief,
    Then the breaking of the spell
    Is the bursting of the shell;
And through the flying fragments flits the phantom .... THUNDERSQUEAK

Are Change and Rest two spirits in a cocktail of delight?
Or are they two mad demons, a-fighting for your life?
    When you reach to touch the stars,
    And all you feel is .... bars
In the gaps between the atoms slips the trail of .... THUNDERSQUEAK

'Unity is Strength' they say – but what controls the unit?
Parts of that machine are we – and who is free to prune it?
    The machine is now a brain, we see
    Its dreams are those of .... tyranny,
But the friction in the bearings is the power of .... THUNDERSQUEAK

'Reality' is 'Royalty' – let us bow before the One;
But let him not forget 'twas we who placed him on the throne.
    As creators of Reality
    We too can taste divinity,
But the aftertaste that haunts you is the demon .... THUNDERSQUEAK

    Oh, Thundersqueak, my Blundersqueak,
    My give in - but don't go undersqueak
    While heavy hands reach to catch you, and close on emptiness,
    On the open palms of the joyous you never cease your dance

       THUNDERSQUEAK!

                (from The Ballad of Thundersqueak)

PREFACE

At first glance this book appears to concern itself with politics; look again and it is a book about magic. Johnstone once replied to a critic who had been shocked to hear him apparently preaching political extremism that there was no point in his speaking in alchemical riddles, because we "no longer participate in chemistry". Having just come across Owen Barfield's excellent book 'Saving the Appearances', I found this half-remembered conversation assuming greater significance. For Barfield begins by suggesting that mankind used to participate in nature and has since evolved into thinking objectively about it.

In case any readers have not come across Johnstone's theories of magic, introduced in 'S.S.O.T.B.M.E.', I will summarise them here. But to save repetition I will describe them in terms of 'participation', rather than the terminology used in 'S.S.O.T.B.M.E.'

What is understood popularly by the word 'magic'? It is surely some idea of willfully defying the laws of nature. One imagines a savage observing his parched land, considering the difficulty of adequately irrigating it, and so deciding to do a rain dance ritual in order to make it rain. Whereas irrigating the land would be 'technology', the rain dance would be 'magic' because it would mean changing the weather by will, and this is 'impossible' because the weather is quite independent of one's will.

Now, according to the theory of 'participation', this picture is misleading; for the savage does not, in a cool and detached manner, weigh up the merits of 'trying out a rain dance'. In fact he 'participates in' the elements and his environment, that is to say he thinks and feels at one with them. The sequence 'drought, discomfort, rain dance, rain' is as unmiraculous and natural to him as is the sequence 'full bladder, discomfort, going to w.c., urinating' is to us; because the savage does not have this idea of being separate from the elements and so of their being 'independant' - an idea that we take for granted.

'Where there is participation there is magic - but no miracles'. That sentence gives the essence of Johnstone's view of magic. He suggested that when we were at one with some world view, or 'belief', then phenomena would tend to conform to that belief. To him 'magic' was something very basic and natural and that it only eluded us because of its modern, erroneous, association with 'doing the impossible'. The coming of rain after a rain dance could not possibly seem a miracle, or be a surprise, to the savage because that would suggest he did not believe sufficiently in his dance before he did it. Johnstone's theorem is that 'unity with belief implies a world conforming to that belief' and he saw exceptions to the rule as pathological, and able to be explained away in the theorem's own terms. For example: any attempt to scientifically test the efficacy of savages' rain dance rituals would be biassed by the experimenters' own beliefs. The fact that scientists would disagree, seeing the exceptions to Johnstone's rule as the norm and the concurrencies as otherwise explicable, simply serves to illustrate his rule: the world will conform to the scientists' beliefs just as graciously as it does to Johnstone's.

Barfield suggests that there has been an evolution of man's thought away from participation towards objective thinking. At first sight one is tempted to regret this, but he points out that the development of science would have been impossible without such a detached viewpoint. Nor is this our only gain. For example it is our detachment from nature that allows us to 'love' nature and cherish it. This would hardly be possible if we were still total participants in nature, in the same way that an unborn child cannot be expected to express what we call 'love' towards his mother. Moreover Jung's VII Sermones (quoted in this book) insists that man must "distinguish himself from Creatura". So this withdrawal just _must_ be progress!

But if we have achieved this detachment, and we no longer participate, then why is the VII Sermones preaching to the already converted? Again Barfield points out that the evolution is still far from complete; it is easy to forget, or overlook, the extent to which we still do participate. The VII Sermones speaks of sexuality as an independent demon who visits us when he will. This accords well with detached observation. But how easy it is to forget this and to identify with 'our' sexuality, and how many people suffer torments of self doubt as a result! Indeed we can say that the universal distinction between 'subjective' and 'objective' is in fact a division of the world into participated and non-participated phenomena.

Troubles arise when we muddle subjective and objective. A woman pampers a child with her love and at the same time is afraid of 'spoiling' it. If it turns out egotistical she is full of remorse. Yet her horoscope shows her to be naturally over generous, and her child to be naturally egotistical. She is upset because she thinks "IF I had been stricter ...". But unless she had achieved a level of detachment that is still extremely rare such scientific thinking is utterly out of place: any attempt to act against her nature would merely have produced strain. When halfway out of Eden the only freedom would seem to be the freedom to make mistakes.

Whereas we no longer participate in physics or chemistry there is still an element of participation in medicine, and a whole lot of participation in psychology, politics and such 'follies'.

Picture a middle aged man - no, a judge, it makes a better story - whose sexuality no longer flowers in his wife's embraces. Instead he goes once a month to a Soho flat where he dresses in a rubber Billy Bunter outfit and is whipped by a prostitute in a leather gym slip and thus experiences sexual ecstacy. In the eyes of a being who had achieved this total separation from his sexuality, seeing it as an autonomous demon, this performance would appear every bit as magical as a conjuration of Lucifer, or the invocation of rain. In place of our ability to perform such 'magic', this being would boast a precise technology of sex. But in our eyes such behaviour is not magic, for we participate in sex. However, the example is instructive if we can see it as magic, for it well illustrates the 'energised enthusiasm' described by Crowley as necessary for magical work.

The modern school of magic is very much an attempt to create this 'inner' technology. Subjective states are separated, or 'objectified', as 'demons' or 'spirits' and are thus brought under the control of will. Psychology, in its many forms, tries to do the same. But Johnstone felt that neither of these had sufficient support from the group mind in this century. He reckoned - back in the sixties - that the clearest and most complete objectification came from the idea that all our 'inner' states were chemical changes in the brain. So he felt the future 'inner technology' would be on such lines.

Now such a future for mankind I find depressing. The idea that love and hate will be tamed, that we will have to swallow one pill to put us to sleep, another to wake up, another to make love, another to get angry - such an idea brings me no joy. "So what if it doesn't?" asks the cynic, "so long as it's true!" But this is a very curious idea of truth. Johnstone argued that the pioneering days were over and we no longer needed such a puritan concept of truth. That the truth could ever be boring was to him utterly ridiculous, as he had adopted the definition "Whatever belief brings the most inspiration and joy, that belief shall be called the most 'true'". So if we imagine two people, one a hard-headed 'rationalist' who believes man to be a naked ape and who turns to drink in his old age, and the other a dear old lady who believes that we are all floating in a vibrating ocean of God's love and who dies with a smile upon her face, then there would be no doubt that the spiritual score-card would read 'Dear Old Lady - one: Mister Hardhead - nil'.

In this case we must take another look at this depressing future. Would it be true to say that the less extensive is our participation, the more intense it becomes? That the smaller the territory claimed by the ego, the more fiercely it is defended? So that it will be harder for us now to objectify, say, politics, than it was in the past to objectify, say, chemistry. Is it not also true that the retreat of participation is a retreat towards abstraction? So the tendency now is no longer to participate in some inanimate object, nor even in a family, or nation, though some still participate in a 'race', but now we are left participating in ideologies or theories. So if we ever withdraw to the point of becoming totally robot-like, then it will mean that although we will have apparently obliterated participation, there will be one invisible exception - for in a totally predictable world we will have become totally identified with the theory of causality and material existence. The political analogy is that there is a tendency in a democracy for power to condense into fewer and fewer hands and to converge unobtrusively towards totalitarianism. The revolution that will overthrow this ultimate tyrant is the concern of later chapters of this book.

What, then, is the future of magic? At present those of us who feel frustration and the need to rebel against the tyranny of materialism are hampered by our search for the miraculous, the desire to shatter the materialist smugness by 'doing the impossible'. For every miracle we witness is later refuted or explained by science and so strengthens the materialist case; just as every new artistic outrage intended to shatter bourgeois smugness comes to be accepted and absorbed by the bourgeoisie itself. Johnstone suggested that this popular idea of magic, as 'doing the impossible' was not what lay behind the ancient practices which we also choose to call 'magic'. For unless one has the idea of being separate from the world, direct action on the world is no miracle. Unless one has a law, one cannot break the law. Until there is an establishment there can be no revolution. So deep is our identification with the basic tenets of materialism that those of us who are not happy with them are like those who realise that their emotions are a problem and wish that they could get rid of them, or the savage who first realises that the weather is a problem, and wishes he could become independent of it. We have a long way to go.

Many of us get stuck in 'low' magic. Though not harmful in itself, it is a distraction if such dabbling serves to disillusion us. 'Low' magic is to withdraw oneself a little from the strictly scientific world view, into a belief that allows a little more freedom. There we perform our 'magic' before returning to the ordinary world. This was described in 'S.S.O.T.B.M.E.' where the word 'feeling' was used to describe participatory thought. Disillusionment comes from the mistaken desire to alter the actual scientific world in this way - an impossibilty as a scientific world that allowed itself to be altered magically would not be a scientific world. If we attempt to 'confound the sceptics' by such magic we will only find ourselves 'explained away'. Not to realise that this is inevitable is to become disillusioned with magic and confirmed as a materialist. The political analogy is of the wise tyrant who constrains youth in schools with a very rational disciplinary structure, so that the people who have worked off their rebellion in youth will mature to realise the foolishness of their ways. (While schools riddled with absurd disciplinary restrictions foster individualism by encouraging cynicism about systems of law.)

The hopelessness of trying to overthrow science by low magic is what dooms those who seek salvation in parascience. Science will only extend itself when ready to do so, and any new territory gained will be as heavily policed as the old territory.

Only after the revolution will we see that science's greatest achievement was that it shewed us how properly to do magic. When we can form our own beliefs consciously and live them out with the intensity of a dogmatic materialist, yet without thereby succumbing to the dominance of that belief, then we will be as Gods and Creators.

This is the revolution this book is concerned with. Mankind is still evolving - we no longer participate in chemistry but we still participate in politics. Instead of alchemy we have alpolitics to link the 'inner' and 'outer' worlds. As the membrane of consciousness that separates the 'inner' from the 'outer' shrinks inwards, alpolitics too will begin to fossilise and this book will become a collectors curiosity!

Until that time I hope these notes will help others to appreciate Thundersqueak. I would also like to thank everyone who has helped us in any way with this book - that includes all those who expressed their appreciation of S.S.O.T.B.M.E. and so encouraged us to try again!

> Ram
> Sea
> Deux.   September 1979

vii

1

INTRODUCTION

T is said that, in times long past, the portals of initiation were built low so that they could not afford entry to the candidate who was not prepared to humble himself, and pass through on his knees.

Accordingly, though the comparison proves flattering, the entry to this our book will be by way of an embarrassing little story.

In 1965 a 17-year-old youth set out on a decrepit motorcycle to find Lemuel Johnstone. He arrived in the village just as the Sunday service was finished, and the congregation was decanting itself into the churchyard. To the eyes of a pimply radical this was a most revolting parade of socialite bourgeois hypocrisy; revolting, yet fascinating like an ant's nest discovered by a gardener. The thought of dropping the name of Lemuel Johnstone - the Destroyer of Gods and Devourer of Moralities - into that flock excited him to rev his bike to a noisy silence and to swagger up to the most stuffy specimen of chinless pomposity that he could see, to ask him if he knew where Johnstone lived. Whereupon the little man beamed, introduced himself as Lemuel Johnstone, and asked for a lift home.

Our coffee-bar cowboy must have betrayed his surprise and dismay for Johnstone looked him straight in the eyes and said with a smile that could not be seen, but only felt:

"What some people call hypocrisy, I call freedom of spirit".

Now, wasn't that excruciating! Didn't it make you recall your

1

INTRODUCTION

own teenagerhood and wince? No? you were not embarrassed? My God! I don't think you can be sensitive enough to understand what's coming, so must be driven off with heavier weapons.

Socialism makes me puke. I'd love to put the clocks back, better still the calendars. Even Apartheid wouldn't worry me so long as it was policed with a sense of humour. The state can go hang itself. The traditional public school education was good preparation for life . . . . .

Oh! ouch! help! Now we've really got some explaining to do . . . . .

2

WHY I AM NOT RIGHT WING

HOW terrible are the masks that publishers force one to wear in order to make a sale. I would hate anyone to think I was a right winger. Mind you, there were times when I mistakenly thought so myself, so I had better explain how the misunderstanding arose.

In the distant past I asked my nanny as she dandled me on her knee what was meant by the 'Left Wing', that sinister provoker of Daddy's wrath.

Lovingly she explained to me that there were two ways to run a country. You could have a <u>caring</u> government which was large to protect its people; a government which made wise laws to save its citizens from the criminal element in its midst; a government which regulated its people and expected from them large taxes for its labours. That would be a left wing, or socialist government. Alternatively you could have a bunch of careless go-getters who turned a blind eye, leaving the people to look after themselves, while they got on with all the enjoyable aspects of running a country. That would be a right wing government.

What better way could there have been to convert a young lad, just yearning to break his cocoon of suffocating maternalism, into an ardent right winger!

But what a wicked lie! Now, an older and a wiser man, I have discovered the true meaning of being a right winger: It means advocating more law, more order; a larger police force; laws against immigration; prompt legal action against enemies of the nation; and so on. In fact it means something almost indistinguishable from all that I dread in socialism.

3

WHY I AM NOT RIGHT WING

Does that mean that I cannot distinguish the right from the left? No. There is a slight difference. The right winger would polish his shoes. The right wing uniformity would be smarter than the left wing uniformity. The right wing has the monopoly of style.

So, were I forced to choose, I would still opt for the right. For if we are doomed to being bored to death we might at least do it in style.

But is there no other choice? Is there no-one capable of handling decisions as to where to build the latest cathedral, or who to declare war on next, without feeling obliged also to pry into our private lives? Is there no-one who could govern without meddling? As Lao Tzu wrote:"Governing a large country is like cooking small fish", meaning that the less it is prodded the better.

If neither left nor right can provide such leadership where do we look? Up? or perhaps down?

Would it be true to say that nanny's erroneous distinction is in fact a correct description of the way in which people choose to govern their own inner kingdoms?

If it is not true to say that, might it at least be _fun_ to say that? and to observe how some people are forever peering into their minds, worrying about their motives, trying to control their complexes, whilst others go about their lives with outward gaze refusing to recognise internal problems, acting without pondering?

Note that in the more introverted societies of the far east the initial instructions for spiritual development are biassed towards the cultivation of extraversion, as in Taoism where one reduces self conscious thought in order to react spontaneously to life; but in the more extraverted western societies spiritual instruction is initially biassed toward the cultivation of introversion, as in the teaching of Gurdjieff where we are encouraged to be more awake, and to study the mechanism of our own thinking.

It would be nice to find those who, through the introverted technique of reorganising their own inner kingdoms, had brought them to such perfection that they ran in infectious harmony for ever more; or those who, through the extraverted technique of leaving their inner kingdoms to grow naturally and undistorted by self-

4

consciousness and guilt had also attained infectious harmony.

But do you not in fact find those whose inner muddling drives them barmy, or whose dogmatic ignorance leads to psychic revolt?

Do we deduce that redemption lies between the extremes, and is best found by cultivating whatever is least akin to your own nature?

Has this observation any analogous political relevance?

If so, forget it. For when has moderation ever sold books?

3

WHY I AM NOT AN ANARCHIST

PLEASE, let no–one think that I am so stupid as to set myself up as an anarchist. My views on that aberration are very much those expressed by Simon in 'Uncle Ramsey's Bumper Book of Magic Spells':

"Anyone who claims to be an anarchist is asking for trouble. It would be no less dangerous for a handsome young man upon a cruise ship full of decrepit old nymphomaniacs to claim that he was a sexual athlete.

"The only thing that keeps some governments going is the belief that somewhere, someone might be planning to overthrow them. When they find a person who calls himself an anarchist they will follow him everywhere, interpreting his every gesture as an advance.

"Why is it that every grubby little government that I pass has the impertinence to assume that I can spare the time and energy necessary for their destruction?

"Can it be a hangover from the illusion that we are ruled by governments and people, rather than by philosophies and fashions?"

Friends with more taste than humour react to this in horror. "Would you really," they ask, "if shown to a button which, when pressed, would precipitate destruction (or better still an eternal purgatory of pain) for all governments, administrations, civil servants and other bureaucrats, would you really hesitate to press it?"

Of course I would press it, as would any lover of life. But

6

WHY I AM NOT AN ANARCHIST

the important distinction is that I would not press it conscientiously,
or with hate. Pressing that button should be a casual, offhand
gesture like the absent-minded picking of blistered paintwork when
in conversation.

A more mindful purification merely provides momentum to
the cycle of rebirth.

4

TOWARDS A DEFINITION OF POLITICS

I rather like those books where each chapter begins with a
quotation.

LEMUEL JOHNSTONE

JOHNSTONE defined politics as 'the stench that comes from
a decaying religion'. This is, of course, a perfect definition; one from which a person isolated on a desert island
could eventually deduce the entire spectrum of political theory.

But, being a perfect definition, it is also practically useless. It is like saying that 'Beauty is Truth', a statement which
in everyday life raises more questions than answers (for example
'why are judges not pretty?'). What is needed is a practical,
everyday definition of politics. First we observe that politics is
only manifest in the form of problems. Where there are no problems there are no politics. So we can define 'politics' as 'the
working of political problems'.

Now we need only define 'political problems'. Fortunately
this is easily done and can be verified by anyone by simple observation. We use a method which will prove to be an important tool
in the course of this book: it is to take a common politician's cliché
and to adopt its antithesis as absolute truth. Hence we deduce
that:

A 'POLITICAL' PROBLEM IS A PROBLEM WHICH
WOULD GO AWAY IF IGNORED.

This is so straightforward that it leaves only one avenue
for misunderstanding: that is that people tend to forget that a
political problem is often generated out of a 'real' problem, and

8

they therefore lose sight of the real problem, allowing it to be overclouded by the political problem.

For example the fact that adolescent children tend to adopt appearance and behaviour to upset their parents is a problem in many families. But it is not a political problem until the newspapers find a word for it and stir up television documentaries, parliamentary questions and statements from religious leaders. It remains a political problem until the 'media' grow tired of it. But until that happens too many parents think that they have given birth, not to a son or daughter, but to a youth movement.

5

IN PRAISE OF APATHY

Knowledge is but the excrement of experience: experience it's
own repetition.
AUSTIN SPARE - THE BOOK OF PLEASURE

IN the last chapter it was suggested that we should experiment with the adoption of the antitheses of political clichés as absolute truth. Now, there are certain qualities which politicians feel can be dismissed without explanation, for example naivety, reaction, idealism and emotion. When a politician says that his opponent's argument is 'emotional' he does not feel obliged to go on by saying "and I feel that emotional arguments are irrelevant in this context for the following reasons ....". Instead he assumes that 'emotion' is so inseparable from 'bad' that no further explanation is needed. Sure enough we find that in fact naivety, reaction, idealism and emotion are, far from being bad, rather endearing qualities and it is hard not to fall in love with those who possess them. Accordingly it seems a good idea to take a new look at another politician's hate-word, that is 'apathy'.

What does 'apathy' mean in political usage? The dictionary does not help because it describes apathy as a 'want of feeling' and this could hardly apply to those who do not turn up to the polling booth because there is a good programme on television, because they have fallen in love, or because they can see through the candidates. No indeed, apathy to a politician means 'not getting excited about politics'. Is there any more noble virtue?

Hooray! we've found a new virtue! What do we do now? Praise it from the rooftops? improve its image? launch an advertising campaign?

10

IN PRAISE OF APATHY

No, this is the politician's approach: to lumber an idea with associations, to cover it with tinsel and trash until the original idea is lost beneath a mountain of baubles and myths. Instead we must clear away the debris round our discovery so that it can be better observed. We must strip away the dirt with which politicians have smeared and fouled our treasure. For example there is the myth that it was apathy that got Hitler into power. Has anyone ever risen to power on a wave of apathy? Once again the political myth is the exact opposite of observable reality. Anger is the only source of political power. Apathy, like entropy, corresponds with diffusion of power. One does not need to study history to be able to guess that the antics of Hitler's loudest opponents won him a good few votes. Indeed it is usually unnecessary to study history for any purpose: history, like all collections of facts, is just a junk room for muddled thinkers. I may perhaps insult your intelligence by explaining why this is so later in this book.

Thus must we always proceed: stripping away the myths, dirt, and irrelevant associations until there stands before us the idea in its purity, our Celestial Apathy. But here is a temptation, to name it thus. No, we must stick to the original word, 'apathy', or else we will have merely created a new idea in an already over-crowded world, a new distinction between 'apathy' and 'Celestial Apathy'.

6

CHOOSING LANES OR LOSING CHAINS?

If any property is transferred which is mortgaged, the new owner may lift the mortgage at once if he wishes, but he must pay 10 per cent interest. If he fails to lift the mortgage, he still pays 10 per cent interest and if he lifts the mortgage later he pays an additional 10 per cent interest as well as the principle.

RULES OF 'MONOPOLY'

Whatever are the chains that bind us? They are many and diverse. They are best understood by considering other people's chains, and laughing at them. We can order these chains on a ladder of increasing severity, starting with those that seem absurd and illusory.

"Oh mummy, I can't be seen wearing my gucchi's to a punk party". How absurd! How risible! and yet some people would 'rather die' than break those chains.

"My dear, I can't wear my ocelot coat to a 'save the animals' fund-raising show". Here we admit that there is an involvement of conscience, but is the distinction really there? If you already have an ocelot coat the damage is in the past. Think carefully, what exactly is the distinction?

"I can hardly go shopping in my swimming trunks!" An even stronger chain. Why? Has it been tested by experiment?

"When the Salvation Army collector calls you can't just slam the door in his face". A funny idea this, especially as the five shillings you give is often just a payment for the right to slam the door in his face.

12

CHOOSING LANES

"You can't just walk out of your job just like that". The
curious thing here is that, unless you work behind lock and key, it
is likely that for many people the normal avenues for leaving a job
are so embarrassing and tedious that the easiest way would be the
unthinkable way of just walking out just like that.

"When your son is dying you can't just walk by". But what
if medical experts told you that you would be endangering his life
unless you did walk by? And yet, on second thoughts why, in view
of the poor record of medical experts, would that break the chain?

"You have to settle your tax debts sooner or later". If the
choice is so simple why do most people not opt to pay later? Why
can't you cash all you own, burn the money, and commit suicide?

Well, what about prison then? Prison is surely different,
it is a physical constraint forced upon you, unlike the forgoing
voluntary restraints.

First you should recall that it is necessary to prove that
the forgoing restraints are in fact voluntary, and this must be
proved not just to ourselves, as objective witnesses, but also to
those who are victims of such restraint. It is no good the rest of
the world telling you that you are free: unless you know it yourself you might just as well be in prison.

Next we should consider the fact that, according to prison
visitors, there are certain regular prisoners who go to prison as
an escape. Lest this should seem utterly absurd it is worth considering what would happen if you gave £50,000,000 to an unsus-
pecting man in the street. There is a very big chance that, within
a few years, he would be living in a large building surrounded by
guard dogs and humans, and a high wall with locked gates. In this
respect it is interesting to note that in America, where the standard of living is so high, one does not feel free to walk back from
visiting friends at night; instead one is encouraged to go by car,
with the doors locked, and not to linger on the pavement; one's
flat is kept locked and is not to be hurriedly opened even if people
dressed as policemen are knocking at the door. But why do people
lock themselves in, and not walk in the parks? Surely if everyone
does that the parks must be empty and safe? No, because
apparently a few people do walk in the parks and they are muggers

and rapists whom the others flee. But to me this is most odd, surely it would be simpler to lock in the few muggers and rapists and let the many just men go free? The only explanations that spring to mind all sound cynical, eg. either the Americans are kidding themselves and muggers and rapists are in fact the majority; or else the lock makers have such power over the public as to be able to enforce the commercially more lucrative alternative of locking in the majority instead of locking in the minority; or else living in prison is indeed the ideal to which most people aspire when given sufficient wealth.

Finally we should ask ourselves what exactly is wrong with being in prison? Why should the state's ability to throw us in jail be at all daunting to us?

If I was in prison I would not be free to take walks across green fields, filling my lungs with healthy air and feeling the good spring of fine turf beneath my feet. So it would be reasonable to calculate the average time I spend each week wholeheartedly pursuing that activity, and allow myself to spend the corresponding time being frustrated in prison. Similarly with other freedoms. But I suspect it would not amount to a great justification of frustration. The chances are that the amount of time spent consciously enjoying the things which prison would forbid would be small. The much greater frustration is surely due to the tendency to spend the rest of the time thinking about what we might be doing. In other words the worst part of imprisonment lies within our own minds. Many people live a life not substantially different from a prison life, but put up with it because they are under the illusion that they are consciously choosing to live as they do, whereas in truth the choice is unconscious.

The one remarkable virtue in being a prisoner is that you are the only class of people to whom the government gives more than it takes (apart from members of the government itself, of course). Prisoners are the only people outside the government who actually gain more than they lose from the government. However the gift is not given graciously.

What is freedom? Is it the ability to do as you choose

14

without hindrance? But if I was in a prison camp with armed
guards I would choose not to make a dash for it, in order not to be
shot. So staying there would be doing as I chose, yet would not
seem to be freedom.

    Perhaps freedom should extend to an ability to choose what
you choose to do? Make a comparison between your own life, and
being in prison, using this sense of freedom. Each day take one
part of your daily routine and deliberately break it. Let us say
that your daily routine involves rising at 7.30 with the alarm
clock, having breakfast, kissing your wife goodbye, catching a
train to work and so on. Then one day you should get up without
the alarm clock; next you should rise an hour earlier (or later);
next day you should miss breakfast; then you should slap your
wife's face and slam the door instead of kissing goodbye; on
another day you should use a method of transport never before
used; on another day you should simply not turn up for work, and
refuse to give any explanation; and so on through your day.

    The point is that it is no good telling yourself that, for
example, you will not skip breakfast because you know you
could do it, but simply don't think it is worth doing; because it
amounts to being unable to choose what you choose to do. It
would be equivalent to the prisoner who lies happily on his prison
bed, saying "I am a magician, and I could quite easily walk
through that wall, but I choose not to because prison life is O.K.
when you know it is voluntary."

    The point of this exercise is not to show you that that
prisoner is wrong, but that he is perhaps onto a good thing.

    Walking across the open country gives you two dimensions
of freedom, the pleasure of that freedom compensating for the
inconvenience of having to cross streams, bogs, and hedges.
Choosing a lane limits you to walking in one direction, but gives
you a smoother journey. Easy passage is itself a form of bondage if it means that you can no longer face a cross-country walk,
but as long as you believe that you have freely chosen your lane
it is a bondage that does not hurt.

    "There is no thou upon the path
    Thou hast become the Way"   (Book of Lies, Chapter 13)

CHOOSING LANES

The cross country walkers are addicted to their freedom; alas it is not possible to walk in two dimensions at once so their freedom is really the freedom to make their own lane. If they now find themselves walking in another person's lane, and they find that frustrating, then they are temporarily less free than those who are happy to walk that lane. A greater freedom must lie beyond.

These four degrees of freedom are an example of Austin Spare's neither-neither rule of four which will be described in Chapter 24. First there is bondage, then there is the freedom to choose a lane and walk it, then there is freedom not to choose a lane. But above all there is the freedom which sees that these distinctions are illusory and is free not to give a damn about freedom.

7

SELF LOVE – THE NEW FREE SPIRIT

Thou shalt love thy neighbour as thyself.
                                    JESUS – THE BIBLE

IVE close to death. Yearn for release. Then all that
happens to you will be a gift of life.
Plan a perfect death, one that would cause no pain. Research
it, obtain the necessary equipment and carry it always with you.
Then when ever you meet some hindrance to your will, when you
think that you have lost your freedom, then offer yourself a genuine
choice: a quick painless death, or not. It is important, however, to
balance the diet. If this death is only considered in such times of
pain it will gather an atmosphere of painful associations and become
increasingly unthinkable. So it is also good to consider it at times
of great joy: "now that I am very happy should I not finish my life,
before any more pain is felt?"
     Lest the idea of death should be fearful as a Great Unknown,
you must find some way of harmlessly approximating to death and
frequently exercising it, so that the open door becomes a familiar
and welcoming window and not a dark hole which breathes chilly
draughts. For example: after a loud sneeze, when your head is
ringing with emptiness, do not shake your head and re-form the
world. Instead be still and hold onto that emptiness for several
seconds more. After vigorous exertion when you collapse,
gasping for breath, do not immediately start planning your recov-
ery but rather let yourself die of exhaustion; relax in the arms of
death; she will hand you back if you trust her. Take several deep
forced breaths, stretch with all your might till you shudder, then
suddenly let go and collapse. Do not breathe,throw yourself to-

wards death, She will hand you back, purged of the world, your head feeling clean and wholesome. You will feel free.

It is not you that has died, it is the world.

You are all that matters, let the world die.

The air resounds with the thudding sounds of fainting socialists: not to want socialism is not to want politics. Nobody wants politicians, but they themselves create a need by suggesting that they are bulwarks against undesirable politics. Socialism tries to find a structure, or state, which can contain us all; one which can care for every person, and every person's every whim. Such a structure would need to be as complex as the sum total of its coverage, so instead it is approximated to by a smaller structure. But a smaller structure must contain loopholes. The socialist does not lop off the defective part in order to simplify the whole, instead he ramifies and complicates it in order to block the loophole. He hopes to create the perfect society which could exist, and cater for, every individual. As an anti-socialist I would like to create the perfect individual which could survive in any society.

"But you are advocating selfishness!" cry the socialists.

Yes indeed. So what?

When I look inside myself and begin to peel away the labels society has plastered over me, then I am carrying selfishness towards its logical conclusion. If you have chosen your lane then you should follow it to its end, if the alternative is to be always worrying whether you should not have taken a different lane.

'I am British.' But if I were to apply for American citizenship it would not destroy me. So I remove that label.

'I am a graduate.' But the amount of time spent exercising that half forgotten knowledge is negligible. Remove that label.

'I am a writer.' ! Remove that label!

And so on. All my most cherished qualifications can be peeled away, even my personal qualities for, at each stage, I ask myself "if this label was removed would there really be nothing left?"

The process could go on forever. Because it appears to be infinite it suggests two things which do not necessarily follow: either I am myself infinite, or else I am no more than the sum of all these labels. But if you take a foot ruler and cut one inch off the end, then cut one half of an inch, then one quarter of an inch and then one eighth and so on, you will have set out on an infinite lopping operation,but however long you continue it you will still have a ten inch ruler. Try it if you don't believe me.

And try lopping off your own labels and you will find that always something remains which is bigger than all you have removed.

What is this huge thing? this core which is so much bigger than the sum total of all society's modifications of it? But society is only the sum of all its possible modifications, or labels, is it not? Not if we choose to believe that society came first and invented its individual members. That is of course the viewpoint that one associates with socialism, 'you are a product of your society, it has programmed you to be what you are'. But the practising anti-socialist knows society to be the product of its members, and therefore smaller than its members.

Is this huge thing God, or is it Human?

If it is Human then it is a very large thing which I have in common with all other humans. If it is God then my observation shows that it has created the world in its own image and so is a very large thing which I have in common with all other humans.

In either case the path of Self Love, unashamedly pursued, has led me to true humanity. No doubt the path of socialism, unashamedly pursued, would lead to true humanity, but so what? The important thing is that I have found a path which avoids bureaucracy and taxation.

8

MEDIA BLUR

The only way to escape misrepresentation is never to commit
oneself to any critical judgement that makes an impact - that is,
never _say_ anything.

F. R. LEAVIS - THE GREAT TRADITION

HEN I was small I used to avoid the newspapers and political
debates and arguments. My friends told me I was stupid,
that it was vitally important to be aware of those forces
which are shaping our lives and futures, and to ignore them was to
allow yourself to be their slave.

But I persisted in my ignorance and find I am in no quanti-
fiable way the worse for it. Most people will admit as much when
pressed, but still feel that from now on it is vitally important to be
aware ..... Snore.

May I recommend that you avoid all newspapers, television,
radio news, political arguments or activity for a year? or however
long it would take to convince you that they are nothing but luxuries?

Now if I were to suggest that they in fact made no difference
to our lives then my dogmatism might prove a challenge. You
would set out on the experiment determined to prove me wrong, and
would of course find the evidence you sought. This, as will be
explained in Chapter 19, is the secret of scientific progress. I
myself will confess that there have been times when life would have
been easier for me if I had known what was happening in Coronation
Street, or whether the government was Labour or Tory, or who was
top of the football league. The object of the period of abstention is
not so much to prove how irrelevant those journalistic phantasies are,
as to prove how much they owe their relevance to our permission to
allow them to take part in our lives.

20

MEDIA BLUR

Reading Tolkien is less escapist than to read novels of the New York slums because Tolkien's works describe a phantasy microcosm which is with the Tolkien fan whenever he closes his eyes, or even when his eyes are open; whereas the New York slums are hundreds of miles away. However, you might as well argue that, to most of their readers, those 'realist' novels themselves outline a phantasy microcosm in the reader's own mind and so they are no more escapist reading than Tolkien. Those people who brag that they know which party won the last general election are like those who speak in a loud voice about the latest 'in' book. They are both onto a good thing, their knowledge gives them prestige. But nothing is given freely, slowly a price is extracted. Those who have read the latest 'in' book have to suffer next year when it is more 'in' not to have read that book; those who know which party won the election are in danger of beginning to <u>care</u> which party won the election.

When you have convinced yourself that journalistic phantasy does not merit the exclusive right to the title 'The Real World' then it is time to start examining journalistic phantasy. It is not necessary to buy the papers – you can usually pick them up for nothing and being a few days out of date makes no difference once you begin to realise how arbitrary it all is. Nor need you buy a television, it is often more difficult to avoid them than to find them.

In the case of newspapers the technique is first to get yourself into the papers, to see how difficult it is to recognise yourself from what is said, and then to assume all other accounts are equal balderdash. A dilution of this technique is to be present at some event, such as a 'demonstration' that is sure to make the news, and to see how true a picture of the event is obtained by your acquaintances who did not witness the event, but who read about it in the papers. Comparing the spirit of the event as experienced, and the spirit of the event as transmitted by the press, will give you a good idea of how much you can rely on newspapers as vehicles for truth.

Next you note that it is normal to read papers which express the same opinion that you already hold, and ask yourself whether it would not have been simpler just to have expressed the opinions yourself. Note also that there is no greater virtue in reading a paper whose opinions are predictably the opposite of your own.

When you read a journalist's 'character assassination' remember that, although the character being assassinated is itself a work of fiction, there is a human being with the bad luck to be associated by name with that work of fiction. Ask yourself how would you be described by the newspapers; would you recognise yourself in that mirror?

In the case of television begin by watching documentaries only on those subjects about which you know a lot. Observe to what extent the medium presents a shallow, distorted and often inaccurate or false vision. Then extend your viewing to other subjects, bearing in mind that the level of humbug is likely to be uniform when produced by a large corporation.

When you have discovered how useless television is for conveying information then take a look at discussion programmes to see how bad it is at conveying opinions.

Television discussion programmes run to a time limit. What sort of meaningful discussion could possibly be completed to a time table? Knowing that time is scarce, each side decides to shout out for fear of missing their chance.

The one positive contribution television makes to discussion is that it gives equal weight to the opinions of ignoramuses as of experts, asking, for example, a star footballer to comment upon the International Monetary Fund. (It underlines that wisdom by not asking the IMF to comment upon football.) This is a valuable recognition of the greater worth of uninformed opinion. I may insult the reader's intelligence by later explaining why learning makes one stupid.

The idea of a discussion programme on television is not to find matched people who together might reach some conclusion, but rather to find incompatible foes. It is just the verbal equivalent of all-in wrestling. This, like stochastic music, may be an aberration based upon a half-understood idea of information theory. Certainly the idea that 'time is money' contributes, because it seems that the argument for justifying this technique is as follows: if any sentence is spoken by A with which B would agree, then it means that B was for a few seconds redundant (a waste of money better spent on someone who didn't agree).

What a surprise it would be to find a discussion which actually got somewhere! Just imagine a television confrontation between Miss Prism of the Festival of Light, and Zap the chairman of the Right Wing Anarchist's Committee for the Promotion of Public Sex. Miss Prism is speaking:

"...... and now at last the silent majority have a voice with which to turn back the tide of filth that has been forced upon them."

Compere: "And what is your comment, Zap?"

Zap: "It is hard to see the justification for the idea of a silent majority having what Miss Prism describes as 'filth' thrust upon them, when in fact most media men admit themselves to being forced to include this so-called 'filth', forced by a public which prefers to buy it. I recall when, as a kid, I first fell in love, or in 'filth' as Miss Prism would ..."

Prism: "I protest! I have never described 'love' as 'filth'."

Zap: "Oh yes you did!"

Prism: "Oh no I did not. I feel that love, and for that matter sex, is a beautiful thing ..."

Zap: "Then why do you try to repress it in films, plays, books?"

Compere: "Yes! Why?"

Prism: "Because I feel this subject is too important and precious to be allowed to be distorted by the media, and forced upon people in perverted forms."

Zap: "Oh nonsense. Sex is fun! sport! Don't we all need a bit of fun in our lives? 'Perversion' is just an emotive phrase used by those who don't like variety. You are the one that would force people ..."

Prism: "How cheap to compare 'love' with 'sport'! Love and sex are very important matters in their own right, very private matters, matters which should be kept private. We of the Festival of Light feel that it is time we unashamedly declared our moral opinions in public. The public wants reassurance!"

Compere: "What do you say to that, then, Zap?"

Zap: "How very curious. Miss Prism considers sex to be

something personal and private and does not like it to be paraded
in public. She is prepared to make an unashamed public moral
stand, attacking us who publicise sex. However, I consider morality to be something personal and private and I do not like people who
parade their morals in public. In fact I am prepared to hold an
unashamed public sexual display in order to attack those who flaunt
morality."

Prism: "Attack indeed, you merely give us more encouragement in our struggle. But it is interesting that you consider morality in the same light as we consider ..."

Zap: "Yes, of course! In the same way your attacks merely
help to encourage us, and to whip up publicity. How interesting."

Compere: "Er ... Let us get back to the subject of ..."

Prism (ignoring compere): "Perhaps we have been both misunderstanding the nature of our opposition?"

Compere: "Miss Prism, you have been described by Zap in
a recent broadcast as 'a prissy spinster meddling in subjects in
which she has no experience.' What are your comments?"

Zap: "Sh!" (Turning back to Prism) "Yes you could say that
the fact that we only really meet via our respective utterances as
recorded by the media leads to inevitable misunderstanding."

Compere: "Zap, you have been recently described by Miss
Prism as a 'foul minded, fascistic, money grubbing exploiter of the
young.' Would you care..."

Prism: "Oh, shut up, please!" (Turning back to Zap) "Yes,
you could be right. Certainly I have never heard your views on
morality before. It could mean ..."

Zap: "It could mean that we ought to be more direct in future.
Perhaps a meeting ..."

Compere: "Er ... Miss Prism! In the Gents, before this
show, Zap said to me 'just you wait till I get that mean old bitch
before those cameras, I'm really going to screw her.' Perhaps you
would like ..."

Zap: "Look, these interruptions are getting irritating. Shall
we adjourn and continue our discussion in more agreeable surroundings?"

Prism: "Yes! Come on." They get up and depart, leaving
the compere spluttering and aghast.

9

DOWN WITH EVERYBODY

Insanity in individuals is something rare - but in groups, parties, nations, and epochs it is the rule.
NIETZSCHE - BEYOND GOOD AND EVIL

MY capacity for loving any individual that I meet is as boundless as my capacity for hating any class.

I hate the rich. I hate the poor. I hate the blacks. I hate the whites. I hate the middle class ..... though that is less easy because it seems to have been a label created especially for purposes of hatred. (for having been told on separate occasions that both the Duke of Edinburgh and the Welsh Miners are 'middle class', I cannot see what class distinction such a boundary is meant to indicate); but at least I can say that I hate the enemies of the middle class, which usually amounts to the same thing.

I hate students, especially radical ones. I hate the working class, I hate politicians. I hate Civil Servants .... The list is endless.

This is surely the technique used by politicians and the press: take any label and load it with hate so that its use may divide the people and create fervour. Just to show how easy it is, let us do it ourselves. Take any collective description at random.

Jaguar Owners

Aren't they awful? Those jumped-up, used-car salesmen who've not quite made enough to get a Rolls, who rush about in their Burton Director's Suits and Playboy Club cufflinks, taking brassy girl friends out to expensive bad restaurants and always ordering steak and chips and the most costly wine on the menu, who are on your tail in the fast lane flashing their lights when you have only just started to overtake a string of lorries .... and so on. It's easy to hate Jaguar Owners.

Having charged up this battery of hate we can then make use of it. Let us say we are reporting on a disagreement between a landlord and tenant and we want to smear Mr. Jones the landlord, then we write 'Jaguar-owning landlord Sid Jones (42) .... ". Now the readers are so revolted by the idea of this smarmy go-getting spiv of a landlord that it never occurs to them that Sid Jones might in fact be a lovable eccentric who cycles to work each day to save money to pay for meat scraps for his Pussy, an old tame jaguar which had been condemned to retirement from zoo life and on whom dear old Sid had taken pity.

This example is important, it is the key to the instruction in the last chapter to remember that the cardboard hate-targets described by the press have the same name as a human (unless the reporter got the name wrong too).

Journalists are either morons, or else have received some education. In the latter event they must presumably at some level despise themselves and what they are doing. Having been educated on literary lines they have a deep unconscious yearning to be real writers, to write a novel, say. Because they dare not admit it this impulse, like a neglected child, grows willful and acts independently. Thus it is that all newspaper accounts of incidents are really phantasy stories inspired by the particular incident, but having little bearing on it.

10

SOCIAL VAMPIRISM

The fundamental agony of political power is the government's
realisation that it is not itself that rules men's minds, but rather
the tides of fashion and belief. How can it actually touch the
individual mind? In no effective way is this possible. However,
in a small way, it is possible to meddle. For example, one can
alter by decree the units of measurement. Changing a people's
currency is like giving them foreign money to spend - economics
goes awry. So with other measurements. This was sensed by
the French revolutionaries. Although they could not hope to
achieve any precise aim by changing to decimal units, it was
obvious that it would slightly warp the individual's standards of
judgement and loosen the foundations of the sense of physical
reality. This would produce a subtle atmosphere of unreality,
uncertainty or dissatisfaction which would help to promote the
tendency for revolution. A similar trick was tried to counter the
political apathy of the sixties in Britain. That apathy was a healthy
sign of an awakening consciousness. All a government is doing in
such cases is to stir up the hornet's nest and hope that something
'better' emerges. A sign of desperation.
     LEMUEL JOHNSTONE - OVERHEARD IN A PAINSWICK PUB

POLITICS is a disease of the mind. Creeds and moralities
are parasites and vampires that shrivel us, distort us and
make us grotesque.

Parasites can take two forms, whether the distinction is one
of quality or merely one of degree does not matter, so long as the
distinction is recognised. There are those modest parasites that
merely tap a little of the host's abundance in return for being
decorative, and there are those malignant parasites that cannot

27

get what they want without destroying the host.

Of the former kind we may consider mistletoe and a small eccentric aristocracy as examples. Both do little harm, both add a pleasing embellishment to their host, and both can be cut down and hung up on festive occasions.

To the latter class, however, belong politics and vampires and disease. Tourists too belong to this class. Tourists are always attracted to seeing exotic cultures. But this is not mere curiosity because a much better idea of, and closer insight into, a strange culture could be obtained from a well-made documentary film, than by the average package tour. itinerary. No, the tourist cannot just watch, he has to meddle. He likes to make people stop what they are doing so that he can photograph them, he likes to give sweets to children, or to toss them coins. The same instincts run to giving whisky to the natives, or guns; or to telling the natives that the world was not really spewed out of the sun's belly, but was made by a loony abstraction that once tried to be human and ended up nailed to a cross; or to telling the natives that their two hundred generations of ancestors were wrong to let the chief choose a wife for them, because we have known for all of two generations that he has no right to do this, and we are of course much cleverer.

Why does the tourist meddle? One will say he wants a good picture, another will say he wants to educate the poor deprived natives, another will say he wants to liberate them. But in all cases the effect is the same: the host society is infected, it festers and rots. Think of Red Indians and many think of scalp hunting – but that was a sport they learnt from the European settlers. Think of Pacific Islands and many think of cannibalism – something that did not have any place in that society till after the European invasion had corrupted it. Some sort of gruesome kick is got out of this corruption by the tourist, and a lot of money. The tourist moves on, to find somewhere 'unspoilt'.

This is the same principle as is used by the politician: to meddle and destroy so that the life force of the dying people can be bled into the bloated politician's belly. These foul and diseased vermin glut themselves on our agony. Any form of meddling will suffice, like twisting a knife in a lemon to wring out more juice.

Why do they do it? What do they gain? Anyone who observes

the nauseating filth that 'runs' this country will see that for all
their grabbing and stuffing themselves, they hardly show any
sign of benefit within themselves. It is their tarts and playboys
who look better for their wealth, not themselves.

They do it because they are too sick to do otherwise.
Politicians are just the carriers of the disease called 'politics'.

Political theories provide frissons of excitement, they
give a feeling of 'purpose'. But purpose and excitement are no
substitute for fun. The political addict no longer knows how to
have fun. The extent to which you, dear reader, think that
purpose is more important than fun reveals the extent to which
your mind has been corrupted. The only merit in having a sense
of purpose is that it helps one to have fun. But a sense of purpose
is no guarantee of fun - a misguided sense of purpose can even
lead to frustration - whereas an otherwise purposeless activity
needs no further justification as long as it gives fun. There is
no such thing as a misguided sense of fun, in the way that there
can be a misguided sense of purpose, the only blemish is when
fun is incomplete. For example, fun at someone else's bitter
expense is incomplete, because the possibility of reaction lessens
the total fun potential.

Politics, like science, religion, or any other obsessive
belief, gives its kicks at a price: the price of impaired clarity
of vision. Such beliefs act like drugs, they distort one's vision
of the world to give it an unnatural, exciting aspect. Pain and
excitement merge to create addiction: one who has lived the
thrill of a world which is apparently full of, say, demon Jews
plotting his downfall cannot face to lose his political beliefs and
wake up to find that he is no longer a soldier of light against the
powers of darkness, but rather an ordinary fellow in a world of
well intentioned bumblers. No wonder the addict is frightened of
those amiable people who try to wake him up to reality, no
wonder he curses their 'apathy' - the worst insult that he knows.
Just like the scientist, or the religious fanatic, the political
fanatic falls utterly to his belief, reality is moulded in that god's
image. Experience does not broaden the infected mind, it
narrows it. That is why the most travelled people are so often
the least broad minded, the most experienced people are the most

dogmatic. As in the case of the rabid dog who runs amok and spreads the disease, so too does obsessive belief cause its victims to go out in the world to spread their infection.

11

ANGERFORD ON CRIME

A new creation in particular, the new Reich for instance, has more
need of enemies than friends: only in opposition does it feel itself
necessary, only in opposition does it become necessary ..... We
adopt the same attitude towards the 'enemy within'.
                    NIETZSCHE - THE TWILIGHT OF THE IDOLS

H Lea, you old perfectionist, I've yet to acquire that cryst-
al purity of spirit that would enable me to face the 'Living
Death'. In my weakness I still demand of life a seasoning
of grandeur or pride. So I need to cast my mind back to childhood
to discover how the Bold acquired their status.

Did you not once tell me that you used to award bonus higher
marks to your most attractive pupils when you were a teacher?
And that you did this secretly for two reasons: firstly because such
behaviour was frowned upon as unfashionable amongst teachers,
and secondly because you had heard that such behaviourist techniques worked best at a subconscious level. You quoted the slim-
ming experiments where the humans were rewarded each day that
they registered any minute weight loss, without being told the
actual figures, and how much more quickly the body responded
without the interference of the conscious knowledge; and so, by a
similar process, you hoped to make your pupils grow daily more
attractive. Why, you asked, was such a technique so unspeakable
in teaching circles? Was it not because the profession was drown-
ing in a mess of woolly socialist morality?

You quoted teacher's statements such as "it's necessary to
be very hard on so-and-so because he/she thinks that a charming
smile will make up for homework not done"; and you argued that,

considered as training for real life as you know it, the charming
smile needed at least as much encouragement as, if not more than,
the academic work. The usual defence for school uniforms was
not that they made the pupils look smashing, but because they dis-
couraged flashy dresses from standing out and getting 'unfair'
status. So the cult of the ugly in the young was seen by you as a
projection of the teacher's own diseased moral state: infected with
warped egalitarian ideals the teaching profession was in fact
reversing your method, Lea, it was unconsciously rewarding the
ugliness of youth.

Such political infection is common among teachers, because
the political disease is likely to render you unfit for practical work
and so the invalids fall into teaching. The public school system
began to fail when it stopped encouraging the recycling of old boys
as staff and got in loonies from 'outside'. It began to dawn on
teachers in your early days that the only <u>really</u> useful skills were
learnt on the playing fields - skills of handling people and making
quick decisions - and so, with the characteristic unconscious spite
of the sick, teachers began to play down sports in favour of academic qualifications.

But I digress, the point is this: if you really want to make
an impression you must be BAD. Suddenly the world revolves
around you. Teachers are fascinated by their worst pupils, they
are the only ones they remember. Such rebellion is deemed
'healthy', an ironical usage when I recall that the only way one
could be spared the horrors of school routine was to be frequently
sick.

In this respect the teachers <u>do</u> provide good preparation
for life in a socialist world. For a socialist world is a vast and
unwieldy mass of law, every part of which is designed to catch
the criminal.

But surely it is designed to protect the innocent, you ask?
No! that is mere sloganeering. You try to find a law that
protects the innocent and you will find for every innocent prot-
ected a thousand others are 'harassed. The whole apparatus is
aimed not at the innocent, but at the criminal.

The 'innocent' are just a flock of sheep that are fleeced

by government in order to to get guns to kill the wolves. That is
where the real battle is fought. Government does not spare a
thought for the sheep - they might as well be cows, goats, or a
tank full of plankton culture, just so long as they can be exploited
to provide material for the battle between the insane (i.e. government) and the free.

As a criminal you can revel in the knowledge that the whole
machinery of government and law exists just for you. In the face-
less machinery of socialist government there is no aristocracy,
the aristocrats of the socialist world are the criminals.

Think of it, prisoners are the only people who get more
from a socialist government than they put into it.

12

THE FUTILITY OF UTILITY

Resemble all that surroundeth thee; yet be thyself and take thy
pleasure among the living.
This is that which is written - Lurk ! - in the book of the Law.
                    CROWLEY - THE BOOK OF LIES

MY dear Angerford, in your own romantic picture of the
battle of the insane against the free you overlook the very
real hatred and envy of the government for the populace.
Perhaps indeed the government can respect the criminal as an
equal, but there is no question of ignoring the masses. Anyone
who achieves any position of so-called authority in government
will be fuelled by a deep down despising and fearing of a thing he
calls 'the common man'. To him that 'man' has the freedom of
innocence, of lack of responsibility and worry, and a happier sex-
life. Basically what is recognised is that there could be people
who have not been infected with politics; it is the jealousy that the
sick feel toward the healthy.

The setting up of government, any government, is a
declaration of war upon a people. That fact is incontestable and,
as such, not very remarkable or interesting. But what could be
of interest is to consider whether such a war could ever be finally
won.

So let us imagine the ultimate tyranny, the dream of every
government. We would require the people to be divided into small
communities. In every community there should be a sensitive
detector, in touch with headquarters, on the look-out for any sign
of dissent, or individual revolt. A regular confessional together
with social pressure for individuals to betray each other for their

own safety, and a uniform system of regular indoctrination. An
important refinement is that the masses should feel that authority
has superhuman powers to read their minds for any sign of
rebellion - whether the apparatus for doing this exists or not does
not matter, so long as the fear exists and can drive dissent into
betraying itself.

Here surely is the recipe for the end of humanity? How
could such a power ever lose its grip? Schism amongst the rulers,
you suggest? But what if the chain of terror has no end? the rulers
themselves are subject to the perpetual self-scrutiny of mutual
suspicion?

Have I not described the nightmare that haunts every
anarchist? The final Big Brother society? The end of freedom?

No, I have just described mediaeval society under the grip
of the church.

Ridiculous! you say, how can one compare the parish priest
to the sort of video-camera-cum-ECG—scanning mind-probe that
the future police state will use to monitor society? The answer
is that anyone who keeps calm, does not fall into the traps of
paranoia, and studies the true state of progress of such electronic
snooping devices, will realise just how difficult it would be for any
conceivable electronic system to match the sensitivity of a human
being who is intimately involved in a tightly knit community and is
looking out for heresy. What central unit could ever process the
information and sort out the relevant facts as efficiently as a
parish priest in his own community?

But then you might ask about the slowness of communication.
In those days it took days and weeks for messages to be passed up
the chain of power; surely authority was shackled by not having our
present day telecommunications?

In answer I first point out that what is important is not
absolute speed of communication, but speed relative to the current
tempo of life: the pope's mounted messenger was as effective as a
weapon against revolt in those days, as the 'hot line' is in our
electronic age. Secondly I ask you to observe and meditate carefully
on the following consideration: in our present age of increasing
specialisation it is becoming less and less easy for people to talk

a common language without misunderstanding and confusion. In comparison, can you conceive how great a unifying force must have been the one Latin language that linked the whole chain of command of the christian empire?

Our main fear now is of a government with the entire powers of science at its disposal. But remember that in real terms it is just that fear itself which kills freedom, and what greater power could there be in a religious world than to have God on your side? Whether the populace believes that it is an omnipresent, omnipotent God, or an omnipresent, omnipotent Science that is oppressing them makes no difference. For the real strength of such tyranny lies in its hold upon the mind; and there is no more efficient way of getting that hold than by the mind's own co-operation. Hence the importance to the government of YOUR belief in their powers.

Surely that was ultimate tyranny and yet ..... somehow it crumbled.

Government is only a machine of war, The paradox of victory is that the war machine makes itself redundant, and so it decays or self destructs. There can be no final victory of government over people.

Nice one, Lea. Very consoling for the theorist. It's nice to know, as the mind police cart you away, that in future centuries they will lose their grip. But what we now want is something more down to earth: we want practical advice for those people who want to know how to survive in the age of encroaching socialist tyranny. What do we do as earth rolls into darkness? How do we survive the night? Can we?

Yes, there is a way; a way that can be summed up in two golden words: BE USELESS.

Chuang Tzu told of a tree, a tree that grew huge because it was so useless. It was so bent and twisted that it was no use for planks, the branches were bent and the wood splintery, its fruits were useless. It was so goddam useless that no-one could exploit it; and it just happily grew and fitted in with nature.

Our children are brought up on tales of heroism and

glamour, they are given the incentive and desire to be famous;
poor things, they should be taught to be apathetic, useless and
nice.

Until we are blessed with such education it will be
necessary to find our own way into safety. First think yourself
out of achievement. Do you picture yourself before the cheering
crowds? ruling a huge empire? Forget that dream and open your
eyes! Think of the film stars who commit suicide, the pop stars
who live in the safety of expensive prisons as their voracious fans
prowl outside; think of the tyrants and wealthy industrialists who
live in fear of assassination and kidnap. Why, you can hardly
even open your mouth on television without risking some
threatening letter from some source. Think of the fans who
would crush you with love, or the cranks who would slay you with
hate.

Here is the true egalitarianism! Not the prissy preenings
of some hypocritical politician; but society's natural rejection of
all who leave her to excel or distinguish themselves.

That then is the first step, the negative one, learn to fear
achievement. The next step, the positive one, is to learn to
revere lack of achievement.

Gerald Heard wrote a children's book called 'The Wishing
Well'. It was a parable about evolution, and began with a group
of fish in prehistoric time being visited by an angel who gave them
one, and only one, wish: that they could become whatever they
chose. Over the aeons these fish evolved: first into land creatures,
then mammals, and finally towards man. But the point was that
this evolution was a gradual adaptation towards greater flexibilty,
it involved no specialising or extremes of function. However, at
various points in time, these creatures used up their wish and
became something else. Some, while still fish, chose to be fierce
and voracious - to become sharks. At a later reptilian stage some
of the creatures became snakes, others became birds. Later ones
chose to be fierce as tigers, big as elephants, or to move in herds
as buffalo, and so on. The final division before the present age
was that some of the creatures, now hominid, opted to swing in
trees and become apes. Those who had retained their wish, who

still had the choice over their destiny, had evolved into men. All others had become specialists.

Here was presented an alternative view of evolution. One where man was not descended strictly <u>from</u> the apes, in the sense that if you kept apes long enough you would expect them to evolve into men; but rather that apes, and all animals were men's cousins - more or less removed. Man was like the crown of a tree of evolution whose side branches were the various creatures of the world. So here was a pleasing version of evolution, one that did give man a special place and did incorporate a question: how, if at all, should we use our wish?

This is the positive side of the argument: the spearhead of evolution is the non-specialist. In the past our animal ancestors 'chose' to use their wish to become excellent in some field. Some excelled in size, some in swiftness, some in strength and so on. But their excellence was a trap in that it was paid for by a loss of adaptability. The bird had learnt to fly, to soar above the common crowd, but in so doing his arms had evolved along such specialised lines as wings that there was no chance of ever growing hands. Lions and tigers far surpass the humble domestic cat , yet it is the latter who has the chance of multiplying in a crowded world.

The same is true on the local scale of one lifetime. Anyone who specialises and becomes expert in some field, whilst a shining example in the eyes of popular opinion, is in fact an evolutionary drop-out, a falling star.

Unconsciously this is recognised by the group mind of society; and that is why these 'great' men lead such hellish lives.

And that is why the key to survival in the tyranny of the near future will be uselessness. It is the hopeless and innocent simpleton who rules the world.

Any talent you possess will merely attract the attention of government, because any talent can be exploited. If you are strong you will die in battle, if you are clever you will be made to work, and then killed in times of fear: it is usually the intelligentsia that are slaughtered by nervous governments.

Ideally we should be perpetually recieving dole. There are basically two forms of dole: one is to be a civil servant, the other is to receive unemployment benefit. It is the second form that is

38

THE FUTILITY OF UTILITY

here recommended. Being a civil servant gives you too much
money, and it is hard to remain inconspicuous when draining the
country of so much wealth. What is more one is forced to sit and
do nothing all day, whereas the unemployed are free to wander
around and be nice.

Niceness is the third great secret. First we learnt to
fear achievement, next to revere non-achievement; but yet a
slight dissatisfaction persists. What of the weak souls who have
not yet purged themselves of fighting spirit, those who are not
content just to remove their support from the system but actually
wish to hurt it? Niceness is the weapon of destruction and it is
also the third ingredient of survival.

It is niceness that really buggers up the system.

The system can cope with the surly rebel; when you frown
and curse in the dole queue the system loves it; because that,
according to the work ethic morality, is what you are supposed to
do. When you tear up your forms and spit in its face, the system
snarls with glee and bares its claws.

Instead you must be nice: try too hard with their forms, and
get all in a muddle. If you've really got guts you can burst into
tears in the arms of a bureaucrat and beg for his pity: the system
will grind to a halt. It is humanity that clogs the machine, nice,
vague, woolly and cosy humanity. In answer to their cold,
impersonal forms you must write great big woolly friendly
rambling letters until they love you till it hurts. In this way you
become a real dead weight in the system: on the surface too harm-
less ever to attract the attention of the disposal squad, but
underneath a real spanner in the works.

Classification is power, to a bureaucracy. If you have any
outstanding quality it will be your 'label', a hook on which to hang
you, a pigeonhole in which to imprison you. But the utterly
undistinguished nobodies will form an ever mounting pile of
unfilable papers which will be forever mislaid.

With practice you can even reach the point where you can
join in with mob enthusiasms. When the call goes out to join a
demonstration, or to go on strike, don't draw attention to yourself
by opting out, but join in wholeheartedly. By now you will be such

a complete non-entity that your very support for some cause will
somehow stifle it and cloud its glamour.

For no ideal is worth dying for. Once I used to believe I
was prepared to give my life fighting off a Russian invasion, it
seemed a small sacrifice to save England from a secretive and
deceiving government. But then I worked for the GCHQ of the
British Civil Service and discovered that we already were in the
hands of a secretive and deceptive government, one that was not
yet as brazen as the Russian model, but was merely biding its
time. So why should I struggle against outsiders, when the battle
was already lost within our own territory? The distinction between
good and evil government is based on misunderstanding: a 'good'
government is simply a young, immature and incomplete government. It is like the early days of addiction, when the drug is still
giving more than it takes. In politics there are no limits to
degradation - if the enemy uses brainwashing, torture, nerve gas,
nuclear weapons, bacteria, lies, or whatever; then our own
government will use them too, or else will feel helpless. However low a political opponent, you cannot win a political victory
without going lower. What country ever took to arms except in
the name of defence? Any country that ever admitted to starting
a war was a country innocent of politics.

Who should we really admire? the man or woman who is
tortured to death in an enemy prison because he or she refuses to
surrender beliefs, or the person who recognises that ideals which
set nation against nation are the real enemies of mankind and so
is prepared to sacrifice ideals? It is the latter group, the despised
'quislings', who will in fact live to propagate the species, and just
as well. It is only the freaks and loonies who fail to recognise the
enemy troops for what they are: fellow humans suffering a common
disease, the disease of politics.

Once again nature takes care of her own, good health has
its own defences against disease. But why then do we wallow in
our ideas of achievement, of status, of heroism and of glory? Is
it not hypochondria that makes us so?

Think again of that tree of evolution, the straight upward
trunk with its crowning glory as the truly common man, featureless,
nice. All around him lurk centrifugal temptations to lure him off

the upward path; his colleagues one by one fall to specialisation.
Specialisation is to sacrifice yourself for 'what you are best at'
whilst refusing to admit that you might in fact be best at being
yourself. This specialisation is a process of falling for a label,
the temptation is to become 'someone' or something'. Government gives every encouragement to make sure everyone does
become something, has an occupation which can be small enough
to be described on a form. Government cannot handle humans,
as we saw above, it can only handle labels. If you are a rebel
they can take it, if you are a nice bumbling all-rounder human
they cannot. So the system educates us towards committing
ourselves; encourages the young to 'stick up for their principles'
and to excel.

Whether viewed as an inner or an outer process this can
be seen as a battle of life against its enemies. The uncommitted
man is despised as a concept: as a label it does not match against
the labels of success or distinction. But as a living reality he is
feared and revered. When the specialists stop their desperate
struggle and look back to what they have lost, they so often feel
awe in the presence of that amiable uncommitted all-rounder:
the man or woman who has saved the vital freedom for the
future, who still is brimming with the power to adapt.

This is why the specialist reacts with contempt, or horror,
or fascination as he struggles to understand the so called 'common
man'.

I said this process can be viewed as a battle of life against
its enemies, but please don't do so in case it makes you want to
take sides.

Don't get excited, hide your lights under bushels, go
underground, but do it <u>invisibly</u>.

'This is that which is written - Lurk! - in the Book of the
Law'.

13

A NOTE TO FUTURE TYRANTS

To talk much about oneself may also be a means of concealing oneself.

NIETZSCHE - BEYOND GOOD AND EVIL

GOOD day, tyrant. You have just come to power, or so you believe. You have been handed a file labelled 'Potential Subversive Elements for Investigation and Elimination'; and in it you have found my writing, with a memo to the effect that its author could be a dangerous destabilising element in an ordered society, and asking your opinion and what action you wish to take.

May I suggest a good course of action? If you give me a small cottage with a vegetable garden on an island with a good climate and sweet female companionship, I promise not to bother you; why, I might even write some articles in your praise!

Why do you fear to do that? You are not used to people who keep their word? Surely you cannot think I really believe what I have written in this book? That is absurd! I have made it quite clear we should not distinguish ourselves and yet here I am writing a book - can't you see it was all just a joke and it was really you I loved all along?

Oh dear, you poor tyrant, you are not a free man. You are not free to leave me alone because you are yourself tyrannised by pride and fear. What is more you failed to understand what I wrote about the mediaeval church's grip on mankind, the victory that failed. Let me describe your dream, I know it so well.

As you study these files you believe that Science is on your side and can solve all problems. Your police are busy issuing

42

identity cards for the population and secret computer files are
being prepared. Scientists have told you that as long as you can
collect enough information about the population you will be able to
predict it utterly. Your file contains facts about my intelligence,
my stability, my extraversion, my love life, my reading tastes,
my political leanings. Now you think you know me. No you don't!
What you hope is that your brain police know me. But they don't
either; what they hope is that I will be frozen into inactivity by the
<u>fear</u> that they know me.

Now I have got bad news for them: I do not fear. Indeed I
eagerly gave them all that information of my own free will. As
you see from my files I have worked for the Civil Service and I
have worked with computers: that experience was the only way I
could learn a vital fact. The fact is that, whatever the scientists
say about progress, whatever the ideal of a streamlined flow of
memoranda in a super bureaucracy, in practice it is always the
same: too much information buggers up the system.

Not only have I told you too much about myself for your
machinery to handle but also, because I have refused to be a
specialist, refused to be absorbed by a label, it means that my
potential is so wide that I have at the same time told you very
little about myself.

Study all the facts about me in that memo for 100 years
and I will still be able to surprise you, because none of those
facts are enough to pin me down.

This annoys your scientists. They now have a new super
computer with one thousand times the capacity of the old one.
They are going to ask you to insist on knowing more about me: my
chromosomes, my metabolism, my ECG brain waves, my sleeping
habits etc. etc. etc. All this will be fed into the machine, Then,
they assure you, you will know all about me and be able to predict
my every move.

But can you see the mirage they are seeking? They believe
that if they were given enough facts about me, or any other
potentially dangerous person, then they could model that person
inside a computer, and so gain absolute power. From earliest
times the chief's sorcerers have been making models of his enemies

with just that aim in mind.

Here we have a parting of the ways: whereas I <u>choose</u> to
believe that I am a free spirit, that no finite amount of information
will ever truly describe me, your scientists are <u>slaves</u> to the
belief that, given sufficient data, they could produce an infallible
computer model of my behaviour patterns. Thus they hope to
predict my every move.

But surely there is a built-in paradoxical snag: if they
succeed in creating a computer model of me, then they will have
not one but two rebels on their hands. How can their computer
simulacrum of me be a total description of me unless it possesses
its own consciousness, its own ability to understand the situation
of its creation and its own ability to sabotage the system with
deceitful responses to input stimuli? In effect, how could they
ever rely on the monster they have created? If I am only the sum
total of all their information about me then, by assembling all
that information they will merely have re-created me. The rebel
can breed indiscriminately within their own memory banks.

By this paradox their method is its own defeat. The
common man remains free whilst you have surrendered to a false
god called science.

So you must try another dream. You dream of killing me?
No, as George Orwell revealed in 1984, that is not enough. You
wish to torture and brainwash me until I love you, until the rebel
has become a supporter. For you recognise that the enemy is not
in my body, but in my mind. But if the enemy is in my mind
what happens when I am brainwashed and tortured? When my
body's behaviour changes to please you, how can you be sure that
it was the enemy that has suffered or been destroyed; how can you
be sure that it is not merely a spirit that has been driven out?
You have not hurt the rebel, you have merely caused it to vacate
my body. The bird has flown; but at least you used to know, or
believed that you knew, where the bird was. Now it is beyond
your grasp. The bird has flown.

Now I can tell you one place where that bird is secure.
It is secure in your own mind.

Think carefully of other tyrants trying to eliminate their

A NOTE TO FUTURE TYRANTS

ideological foes: The strict inquisitor looking for heresy, the nazi hunting out 'unhealthy ideals', the redneck seeking to eliminate 'un american vices'. How do you know what it is that you are looking for?

If the inquisitor was totally absorbed in his love for Christ he would have no comprehension of, or recognition of, heresy. It is only because that heresy has an existence in his own mind that he is able to see it in others.

I have been shocked and outraged to hear films described by the pro-censorship anti-porn brigade. But it was a revelation once when I later recognised one such film as one I had seen myself. Whereas the film itself had not repulsed me, the description of the film had done so. The repulsive element had been added by the choice of words used in the description. As an unwittingly impartial observer I had witnessed the creation of porn. The porn had come from the mind of the anti-porn propagandist.

As a tyrant you will spend your life pursuing potential enemies. But it will all be in vain. For the enemies that haunt you, and the only ones you will ever recognise or comprehend, are those enemies that already exist in your own mind. Destroy the whole world and they will live on within you. Reduce me to an empty body and what will you have but an empty body? The bird will have flown back to its nest in your own mind. You are the only rebel. there ever was.

Only the innocent are free of such enemies. That is why I preach the death of politics - without really meaning it, of course.

14

THE DIABOLICAL PACT REVISITED

But as for such a matter as the difference between the German and
French Ministers for Reconstruction, and whether you agree with
the arguments of one or the other - all that is mere twaddle. It is
neither here nor there for one who wants to take a serious part in the
progress of civilisation. The fact is, both are untruthful. The only
thing that concerns us is to discover how it has come about that one
of the said ministers is untruthful in one way, while the untruthfulness of the other is of an altogether different character. The
difference of character and outlook that reveals itself in the two
kinds of untruthfulness - that is important.
STEINER - SUPPLEMENTARY COURSE VI

MAGIC is the technique of controlling demons.
I should apologise for that rubbery statement: first one can
squash it, if you know anything at all about magic and its
true scope; next one can make it spring back into shape, if you have
the imagination to extend the definition of 'a demon'.

Right now such debate is irrelevant; let's just admit that
controlling demons is done by magic and get on with the story.

Mediumship is being controlled by demons. Well, let's
leave it at that.

Magicians are very scornful about mediums. They set out
on a very different course but, in so doing, they are in danger of
falling into the same trap.

In theory there ought to be two sorts of politician. There
are of course the usual sort: insane, half witted, possessed, sub-
human morons who really believe their rabid slobberings. But

46

let us conceive of a different sort, ones who set out to manipulate the forces which sway other politicians.

Before you can control demons outside yourself, you must learn to control them within: how can you manipulate hatred when you are yourself in its power? So our embryo political magician must set out to cultivate absolute callousness in his youth.

Perhaps he begins by ripping off the limbs of insects: then he must progress to slowly prising out puppies' eyeballs. It must all become so habitual that he no longer gets an erection as he performs such acts. Every vice and every degradation of human perversity must be explored and re-explored, until there is nothing in the world that does not enjoy the hearty contempt of enforced familiarity.

Allied to this cool cruelty is the need for utter insincerity, a skill best acquired in college debates. One should be capable of arguing for anything from cannibalism to christianity, with the same fervour of simulated emotion. Insincerity is vital; for, if there is any question of caring, then he might get angry and so lose control.

So much for the defences, now for the practice. A magician needs robes. Here there are two lines of approach: either one can devise special purpose-built robes, or else use some existing style of dress which has the correct associations for the work in hand. It is the distinction between an act of creation or an act of choosing. One can either devise a smart new uniform, or one can opt for robes which have a ready made significance: the cloth cap, the military look, the denim look, the man-in-the-street look.

Then you need words of power. Again there are two approaches, but here it is best to blend the two. One can coin new words, or else fall back on association-heavy words like 'fascist', 'class', ,'alienation', 'purity', 'British' and so on. In either case it is necessary to pile on the associations. An interesting fact about magical words of power - true in all ceremonial magic - is that associations are an asset whereas meanings are a liability. The more powerful emotional associations a word has the more it is like an electrostatically

47

charged capacitor, but meanings are like conducting wires which link a word to other words and so allow the emotive potential to leak away. This is the nature of politician's special words: being devoid of meaning they are insulated and can hold a big charge of emotion.

The process of charging new words is similar to the process of charging a talisman. The construction of the names is analogous to the construction of angelic names (whereby a word was taken and the ending '-el' added to signify an angelic name, producing names like Mikael, Uriel, and so on). For political demons we take some associated word and append '-ism' to produce a name such as 'rightism'. The new word is like an empty capacitor or uncharged talisman, and the charging is a process of evoking traditional demons such as 'poverty', 'oppression', 'evil' and so on to coexist in sentences with the new word.

The climax comes with the ceremonial working at the festival of the ballot box. I am proud to say that I have no idea what happens, but anyone whose life is dull enough is free to extend the above analysis as far as is desired.

One example should suffice: the contrast between allopathic and homeopathic techniques in politics. Allopathy is the currently favoured medical approach: what it means in practice is if there is something 'bad' in the system you prescribe a big dose of its opposite, ie. if you have a cold you are given a big shot of cold-clobberer. Homeopathy is the technique of prescribing a very small dose of something similar; as in vaccination when a small shot of cow pox brings out the body's resistance to smallpox. When suffering a cold you are prescribed a minute quantity of something of a similar nature, and it encourages a bodily reaction to overthrow the cold.

In political terms let us imagine that you have decided that everything wrong with this country is due to negro immigrants. The allopathic 'remedy' is to set up a Ku Klux Klan. The homeopathic one is to become prominent on some race relations board, then very quietly announce that Britain is due for a large influx of negro immigrants. Note the homeopathic technique: this must be announced very quietly at a sensitive moment and

then promptly denied. If you announce it from the rooftops no-one
will believe you; if you stick to your guns you will be proven wrong.
But if you 'let it slip'and then shut up, it will be seen as a 'leak'.
No more effort is needed, the people themselves will convince themselves of the truth of the statement and race riots will break out all
over the place.

The point is to illustrate the process of being a magician as
distinct from being a medium. But here there lies the danger of
deception, for we must now ask why our politician does all this?
If it is all done to the prompting of a blind impulse, he is no
different from the medium who is simply possessed by the demon
of politics.

The chances are that the whole process is gone through in
order to gain power, prestige, or some such attribute. But here
lies the difficulty: one has made oneself aloof and indifferent to the
world, yet one is living for a feeling. Without that feeling of power
one would not act, with it one does act. So that feeling of power can
just dangle a few inches beyond one's grasp and keep one running.
One is compelled to do magic for the essential kick it gives. So
one is out of the frying pan into the fire: the politician has
avoided one form of possession only to fall for another.

Demons either take the mind by storm, or else, when
faced with stronger or maturer minds, they need to induce gradual
dependance in their victims. In this game the ends always justify
the means, and one demon does not mind putting down any number
of his colleagues along the way. Thus we often find that the road
to hell is paved with good intentions, good deeds, and even good
results.

Is it possible to be a true magician and bypass this
seduction? Is there such a thing as the truly conscious and free
political act? To find an answer we must play with the paradoxical notion that sacrifice is the only true freedom. This is the
basis of Angerford's Political Satanism which will now be
described.

What it consists of is a re-statement of the diabolical pact
and it will be necessary, for brevity's sake, to condense the
description given in Uncle Ramsey's Bumper Book of Magick

THE DIABOLICAL PACT

Spells.

The basic problem comes from the observation of, say, the teenage rebel. In an acne-sulky storm he batters at life, throwing his energies into protest movements. And then, in his twenties, we see his fury abating: he marries, he settles down, he is tamed. Now is this a triumph or a defeat? Let us look on the rosy side and see it as a triumph of common sense over rebellion. If that is the true picture why then does the problem recur? The most extreme rebels in youth tend to become the most dogmatic parents and elders, and so induce the greatest rebellion in others.

Does this not suggest an alternative picture? The picture of a parasite with different stages of gestation? The battle for your soul comes at puberty; the parasite grows bloated on your energies and tires you out; you carry it through your life deadened by its weight and it ripens to infect another generation. The clue which suggests that the spirit of rebellion was not destroyed, but merely has retreated to brood, is that our Pillar of Society is still under its spell. He lives with a feeling of awe and fascination; he has 'strong views' about dissent, whereas surely a true victory should give one total liberation from care?

So let us consider our most burning obsessions as parasites that feed upon us. They sap our life. But what happens if, instead, we summon them and bargain with our life?

Here we must pause to draw a distinction between 'life' and 'Life'. The first is a tiny flame in all of us that can be extinguished with a drop of poison, or a cord tightened around the neck. On the other hand 'Life' is something too big ever to be seen in toto, we only glimpse it in times of great confidence; it is the sum total of our whole potential, our joys, our hopes, what we could be and have been.

Now the parasites, let us call them 'demons', survive by taking as much of our 'Lives' as they can manage without drawing attention to themselves; for as long as we do not believe in them they are safe. Exposure frightens demons, analysis destroys them. When you face them squarely and offer them your whole Life, not just the scraps, then you are at a crucial point. So eager is the demon that it is a fine distinction as to who is in control at the

50

moment of pact - you or the demon. Quite simply the demon will
not believe you. In order to shock him into belief you must also
offer him your 'life'. He does not want your life of course, but it
must be offered.

The offering of your 'Life' is the offering of your 'soul',
the offering of your 'life' at the moment of pact is to sign the pact
with your own blood. That is all. Now we must give an example,
but what you must study is not so much the specific example as
the principle behind it. So, if this example does not link to strong
feelings in yourself, what you must do is translate the situation
to one which does pain you; and study the example in its translated
form.

Imagine a teenage schoolkid waiting to see his headmaster;
he is in a fury of anger which totally overshadows all other thought.
He is being punished for smoking; but in fact he is being made an
example of, and the punishment is not strictly 'fair'. So here he
is in the grip of the strongest feeling of his whole life: it is burning
rage at injustice. The strength of the feeling comes from his own
feeling of despairing hopelessness: the head has absolute power,
his parents and society are behind him. The boy is on his own
against the world.

So what does he do? He probably makes some ineffective
gesture of surly revolt. To compensate for his humiliation he
exaggerates the account of his 'heroic' action to his friends, and
goes on suffering that rage. The rage will revisit him at times in
his life, in his early years he will try to express it in action. But
an important element of that rage is the feeling of helplessness
against huge wrong, and it is that helpless feeling which will
conquer. He will live his later years in apparent harmony, yet
forever complaining about the injustice in the world. Each time
he suffers that anger he is giving a little of his Life to it; like a
vampire it is draining his life, but like the true vampire bat, it
takes care not to wake him up to a realisation of what is happening.

The information (so often repeated by his elders) that he
will 'grow out of it' is no consolation. Why should the present
bow down to the future in this way? We all grow out of life eventually, don't we?

THE DIABOLICAL PACT

What is the alternative? Here he is waiting to see his
headmaster, and the thought of utter helplessness and inevitability
has just struck him. Instead of succumbing he turns to face it and
questions it.

He is not helpless. If he were to commit suicide he would
bring considerable embarrassment upon the school and the system;
the more so if the suicide was clearly not an act of hysteria, but a
carefully considered and necessary act. At first the thought is an
hysterical one, it is heavy with taboo. But he must work on the
idea before it works on him. It must be a possibility. The sleeve
of his shirt is long enough to throttle himself on, or his razor
could be used on his wrists. He must set the apparatus up so
that the only thing between him and death is the moment of action.

Suddenly he finds he is in a state of cool calm; what has
happened to the demon? He has offered the demon his 'life' –
a gift not truly desired for reasons that will become apparent.
The demon is silent with surprise.

The boy turns on the demon and asks his name – in the
calm state all is clearer and smaller.

This is the first great benefit of this teaching: a vast
majority of minor demons will flee at this point. When the sacrifice
of one's life is coolly contemplated, a host of lesser demons, that
would otherwise sap one's Life in little sips, will flee rather than
face such responsibility and power. Thus you are freed.

But what if it doesn't flee, but says 'Destruction of Authority
is my name'? This means that the demon is a match for the boy's
life, and it is a match for that portion of his Life there present.
But what a miserable little bit of that Life it is! Here is a human
who could grow to rule the world, all he is now is a snivelling
schoolkid about to be caned.

So the next challenge to the demon is to offer it one's Life.
He should imagine the fullest possibilty of his abilities: imagine
himself in later years at the crest of a successful and brilliant
career, when all he had ever wished for was within his grasp.
Then he should ask himself if he would be prepared to destroy the
whole lot to honour a pact he had made as a schoolkid.

A demon who survives this challenge is Satan himself. So

the boy faces the demon and names it as his Total Desire and
offers it his whole Life and nothing less. The importance of
'nothing less' is that there could be the temptation to make smaller
sacrifices, to give in to lesser bursts of rage; but once you do this
you begin to bleed your Life, and it will never be realised in its full.

The boy thus locks out Destruction of Authority; leaves it
to pace hungrily around the <u>outside</u> of his Life, and never lets it
in until he is fattened for the kill. When the headmaster summons
him he is neither extremely surly, nor extremely submissive. He
is like an ordinary, slightly scared, kid without hangups. By this
time it is not a question of 'acting' that way, but just of allowing
himself to be that way. Being free of this hangup he can pass
through the rest of his education as any 'healthy' adolescent would –
a bit of a rebel but basically level-headed. Just the sort who will
make a good manager.

The boy becomes a very normal person when it comes to
collision with authority, he will show normal signs of anger but
will never suffer that consuming resentment that he would have
felt without the pact.

If some situation is likely to launch him into rage, he
senses the coming storm and slams the door on it before it touches
him. A brief phrase, such as "YOU WAIT!" can help: he feels a
flash of anger and he hurls it from him with that phrase shouted
internally. One can either see this as raw (ie. uncooked or
undigested) meat hurled out to the stalking demon, or else one can
see the demon as a sort of flywheel spinning-top that is given a
whiplash to keep it fast, and so stable.

Because that original rage was the biggest thing in his life,
he has removed the biggest hindrance to his Life, he has abolished
his biggest hangup. So he becomes very successful.

This is quite natural. Destruction of Authority wants to have
as much as possible when it cashes the pact, and so it does all it car
to remove restraint and allow the man to flourish. What is more,
the bigger demons would not make a pact with someone, unless they
knew they could get a lot for it.

And then one day the summit of a brilliant career is reached,
and the demon comes to him pact in hand. If he is a politician then

he could sacrifice his reputation in a war; as a scientist he could defect with military or economic secrets; as an economic adviser he could ruin a country; at the very least he could go berserk and slay all those people to whom his elevated position gives access. The more you have got the more you can give, a brilliant life was gained, a soul was lost. Who can say it is a bad bargain?

Do not feel tempted to believe that you need not honour the pact at the end. One of Johnstone's regular principles was that 'success is a rut'. The times when you really are free to re-shape your life are the moments of depression, failure and emptiness. By contrast success has its own momentum, it carries you along with it. So the cashing of the pact cannot be avoided, and it will come when you have a lot to give, and probably your life will be asked as well.

When so much is given it is not altogether clear why death should also be insisted upon. I can only assume an analogy with fatal disease, and suppose that your death is needed in order to free the demon so that it can spread elsewhere, just as the death of the host body releases bacteria to the air. Various other illustrations suggest themselves: would Christianity ever have gained such power if Thingummybob had not let himself be crucified? Why is it that the conquest of a country seems to infect the victors? (As when the Roman empire, having swallowed the Greek empire, found itself corrupted with Greek fashions.) 'Who won the last war?' is not a very interesting question, but 'what won the last war?' is. So many of the nazi ideals, methods and obsessions are now taken for granted in the world - the people's car, racial unrest, missiles, jet aircraft, secret police, brain-washing, anti-semitism - what would have happened if Hitler had lived? By now he would be on his death bed, and the Reich would be crumbling. Whatever it was that lay behind the nazi movement, it has best guaranteed its dissemination and survival in the world by apparently letting Germany be conquered. Christ and Hitler are the two greatest examples of the vast significance of timely death, the surrender that disguises total victory.

As this book was being prepared there came the news of the Revolutionary Suicide at Jonestown, the most amazing act of defiance in recent years, We have yet to see how far-reaching the effects will be. Certainly it has shocked the politicians who like to believe that they are the only men who can send people to kill themselves. Admittedly politicians can boast of megadeaths, besides Jim Jones' paltry thousand, but what politician has managed so many conscious suicides? Usually they have to resort to trickery and promises of possible victory and medals.

But so important is the timing that one does need the superhuman assistance of a demon to pull off the big one.

Earlier we exhorted you to keep a handy death beside you as a perpetual companion. Here comes the first pay-off: the casual offering of your life in the first stage of diabolical pact is a helpful way of deflating minor obsessions. It provides a yardstick by which all trivial demons are seen in their full smallness. When apparently stuck in a rut in your boring office job you can toy with your amusing paperweight - a lifelike facsimile of a hand grenade - nibble at the pin and see how close you are to blowing that rut wide open, for only you know that the grenade is, in fact, real. Then the whole situation looks different.

But what about the big one? Is tradition right in insisting that there is only one god that merits the gift of a soul? Are we to believe that God created us and that we created the Devil? Should we not then show as much love to our creation as God does to his? Is there any greater sacrifice than to be prepared to forego even the Kingdom of Heaven and enter eternal damnation for the sake of a cause? Don't ask us: the ideas we give are meant to be used and explored, not listened to.

15

SERVILE SAVANTS -
OR
THE BLUNDERING GOONS OF WHITEHALL

The best of all rulers is but a shadowy presence to his subjects
LAO TZU - TAO TE CHING

 H Angerford, you naughty boy! Diabolical pacts indeed!
Smack your bottom! You leave bombs and bullets to the
women and children, my lad, for surrender is the ultimate
weapon.

If you want to beat 'em, join 'em. There is nothing to
match half-hearted support as an extinguisher of fire.

Divide and rule is the method of all political theory, so
refuse to be divided.

Do you recall the police raid, when you dragged me to
Middle Earth one night? We were a room full of people until the
police arrived. One musician made a call for us to unite against
the police: then suddenly the people were no longer people but
'hippies' and the police were very 'police' - I actually saw a grim
faced police woman kicking open doors, and I sort of loved her
for it.

Why, why, why, I asked you, didn't these hippies join the
police force?

Why don't tories join the communist party? Why don't
coloured people join the National Front? Why don't octogenarians
flood youth clubs and slash the seats? Why don't strip club owners
join the Festival of Light? - but perhaps they do?

As Lemuel Johnstone said, "What some people call hypocrisy,
I call freedom of spirit." So become whatever you despise most -
so long as that despising is a nuisance.

SERVILE SAVANTS

Why do people not take advantage of this most economical form of entertainment more frequently than they do? Why don't the humanists flock to church each Sunday for a giggle? One reason, I suspect, is that they are slave to pride: they would be too embarrassed to be seen at church when they are supposed to be anti—religion. In that case they should examine this tyrannical pride with suspicion - if it can make negative demands might it not make positive demands? Perhaps it is only pride that keeps them in the Humanist Association?

In the case of the college revolutionary, who does not want to get an ordinary job and become 'part of the system', another fear is more obvious. It is the fear that one's ideals would not survive in uncomfortable surroundings; that one would succumb and become part of the system in spirit as well as body. Again I would exhort such people to be wary of living their lives according to the whims of a philosophy which is itself too weak to support one. If the nine-to-five job is capable of making you forget your reforming zeal, then the reforming zeal was well forgotten.

This cleaving to one's opposite is like a test of friendship. Those who rebel against authority are often promoted to positions of authority for the simple reason that it 'makes them see sense'. But this 'seeing sense' simply means that their old best friend who was Destruction of Authority has turned out not such a good friend after all. They should be grateful for the revelation.

If their principles do survive the test, then the principles are better for it. If Destruction of Authority can survive in a position of authority, then it will have learnt a lot about its enemy.

Everybody has a duty to join the Civil Service. In every age there is some frontier beyond which lies the challenge against which youth can match and sharpen its bravery and manhood. The new frontier is boredom, and the Civil Service is the most bored and underworked society the world has ever known.

One of those many embarrassing little fibs that emanate from the Civil Service recruitment board (I almost wrote 'bored') is that 'every government needs a line of communication between itself and the people, and the Civil Service fulfills that function'. Now if we apply the old and trusty rule of accepting the opposite of

any political statement, we arrive at the patently obvious truth
that 'every government needs a thick wall of sandbags between
itself and the people, and the Civil Service fulfills that function'.

The Civil Service is such a fruitful example of the evils
that we are warring against, or pretending not to, that it must be
examined most carefully. For a start every man, woman and
child of the realm has a duty to send in at least one bogus job
application per week to the Civil Service. This does not cost
postage - just write OHMS on the envelope - and the time
consumed filling in forms can be quite good fun if you take a
stack of them when you meet your mates at the pub and have a
good laugh over them.

This activity should be continuous; it is a sort of limbering
exercise for yourself; but it also provides something to do for the
dormice at the other end. What you notice is the incredible
amount of information that is being collected, and you begin to
wonder where it all goes. This is the point where you slip in a
genuine application: with a deep breath you make your first step
toward the Big Country. You are about to find out where that
information goes, and you do. The answer is that it gets lost!
You will find yourself dropped into a job utterly irrelevant to
your skills and inclinations - somewhere along the age-long
recruiting process names are taken from a hat. I know of one
person who had to undergo a six-month screening involving three
lots of detailed personal forms of several pages each (and considerable duplication of content), several interviews, intelligence
tests, a four-hour grilling about his morals in his own home,
together with an examination of his friends and acquaintances: and
the job that was being offered was turning the handle of an old
fashioned calculator in a Ministry of Agriculture office!

The emphasis on intelligence and exam results is interesting.
Government fears people of ability, and so wants them removed
from the masses as a potential danger. What better disposal than
to stuff those sandbags with ashes of the intelligentsia? But how
lucky for mankind that government itself is so enslaved by its
worship of form, that it is reduced to using such conventional tests
of ability that anyone of real worth is able to pass unnoticed through

SERVILE SAVANTS

the system.

Once within the Civil Service one is in a position to learn
so much about the mechanics of oppression, it is a university for
the aspiring magician. Study the bureaucracy as a Saturnine
symbol. Saturn opposes change and so there is no concept of job
mobility or change in the Civil Service. Saturn governs the process
of aging and so we find only the concept of 'promotion'. This is a
good example of how the worst tyrannical notions can have the most
benign faces: the fact that the only way out of a particular job
within the Civil Service is to be good at it, and be automatically
'promoted' elsewhere at random is, for anyone who has studied
mechanical sorting methods, a beautifully simple method for
making sure that everyone will eventually come to rest in the
very job that he or she is worst at.

Remember when you see those sour-faced, shy people with
downcast eyes who run the dole counter, that they probably joined
the Service in the hope of getting away from people and into office
routine. Remember when the Ministry of Agriculture produces
inane and worthless statistics that they have been created by people
who joined the Ministry because they liked farm work.

16

THE BIG MEAT

The sense of the tragic increases and declines with sensuousness.
NIETZSCHE - BEYOND GOOD AND EVIL
The maturity of man - that means, to have reacquired the
seriousness that one had as a child at play.

(IBID)

OVERPOPULATION: a word to chill the heart of any right
wing anarchist. Surely this is his Waterloo? His politics -
or rather 'anti-politics' - belong in a small, villagy, world.
Huge populations fall naturally into huge and revolting groups -
students, immigrants, socialists, football fans, teenyboppers -
small communities fall naturally into small and rather charming
groups - young children who know how to stroke cats, elderly
ladies who run teashops, beautiful girls, retired colonels who say
"by gad, sir" without affectation, and solitary craftsmen.

Do we have to admit that our philosophy will have to lie
dormant till some holocaust has fragmented the population, or can
we find some way to banish this obsession like any other?

The solution may just be a personal solution, for it can only
be presented as method and not as dogma - just like all the other
ideas in this book.

So I run through all the images of overpopulation, ie. I
walk around this mountainous obstruction studying its various
aspects, looking for a route. Vast crowded streets - ugh!,
hypermarkets - yuk!, mass rallies - puke!, huge statistical samples
- groan!, endless traffic jams - yawn!, miles of crowded beaches...
miles of crowded beaches? I've found an image that has a sort of

ambiguous attraction; let me explore it.

People flocking together to sunbathe: this was the first image that did not have a suggestion of abrasive bustling. Instead it had a sensuous and pleasurable feel: naked in the heat of the sun one is less concerned with other's proximity; indeed, given a fair proportion of attractive girls the closeness is positively desirable.

That's it! Crowded beaches are sexy! But does that mean overpopulation is sexy? No, I'm not ready for that; it still associates with frustrated and frenzied jostling. So I must forge some sort of link between the sexiness of crowded beaches and overpopulation.

Crowded beaches are sexy because of extraverted people flaunting themselves: girls wearing bikinis that they wouldn't dare wear in their home territory. It's the most charming of all the mating parades. The effect of hot sun on skin seems to dispell that neurotic nerviness which is so undesirable in a crowd.

Reading Eysenck's work on extraversion I see that extraverts tend to have sex earlier and more often than introverts: that would suggest that they are likely to out-breed introverts in the long run - especially as greater impulsiveness and lack of caution would make them less likely to restrict their families. But being suspicious of scientists' self-deceptions means I must check this observation against my own, and it seems unsurprising. Next I must ask if it makes sense.

Apparently the characteristic of introversion is a highly tuned receptivity or alertness compared with the extravert. So the introvert does not seek a lot of sensation, and finds too much noise and bustle confusing; whereas the extravert flourishes on noise and activity. Now man is evolving towards an urban existence, out of solitude and into the crowd. So surely the man or woman of the future would better be an extravert? The introvert would go barmy in a city of fifty million people living on top of each other, while the extravert could appreciate the stimulus. But in our distant past, in a hunter society, it was the introvert who had the advantage. The introvert was the one who could sit patiently for hours waiting for his prey, who could creep undetected through the jungle, cautiously leaving no tracks.

THE BIG MEAT

This then is why, in our increasingly crowded world, nature is breeding us towards extraversion. But a doubt crosses my mind: what of the many girls who say they prefer introverted men? The answer is that, from an evolutionary point of view, it is not who one likes, but who one gives in to that matters.

For a glimpse of just one of the many factors which could promote the change, consider the hospital practice of inducing births to take place in daytime for the convenience of modern working hours. There is no exact astrological correlation with introversion-extraversion, but one of the relevant factors is the relative number of planets above or below the horizon. More above the horizon inclines the native to an outward or extraverted personality. Normally the most common time for a mother to give birth was in the early hours of the morning - before sunrise. Thus nature was ensuring that at least one of the luminaries would be below the horizon at the time of birth, and so biassing the sample towards introversion. But in civilised society we arrange our births for daytime when the sun will be above the horizon, thus biassing the population toward extraversion.

Here is considerable consolation: the overpopulated world of the future will not be a world full of bitter and twisted cruds like myself; it will be a world full of cheerful extraverts because they are just the people who would like that sort of world. So my original dread of overpopulation was based on a false projection: it was the idea of a world full of people like myself, all hating it.

But still I feel sad to think of nature being squeezed out. I think of the locust mentality of those people who say we should not feed our cats on meat while millions are starving. Which would I rather keep as a pet? a nice fluffy cat or some scraggy human being who would probably declare war on me once its belly was full? Cats are so rare and precious: when I see a nice cat I cross the street to stroke it. Would that humans were so scarce that I felt inclined to cross the street to talk to a stranger!

The crowded beach is a good image of the overpopulated world, for the beach is like a desert, empty of plant or animal life, flat featureless sand. The only sign of nature is in the human bodies themselves. Can I really be content to imagine that the beauties of the natural world are going to have to give way to a mountain of scrawny human flesh?

Perhaps the error is to picture ugly humans? Although I far prefer to watch a field of wild flowers to a crowd of nasty people, I would yet prefer to observe a beachful of beautiful human bodies above all.

But surely a similar rule of selection to that already described would tend to make mankind evolve towards greater beauty of form? Why do we believe otherwise?

There is the idea of the beautiful savage from which we have degenerated, and there is also the idea that the people of Greece really used to look like their statues. If the latter was true and the Greeks really did look like that, why would they need statues of themselves? They surely modelled those statues as ideals to which they should aspire rather than themselves as they were?

The beauty of some uncivilised people is largely ascribable to correct physical expression. A body which does physical work grows more shapely; skin exposed to the sun takes on an attractive colouration which obscures blotches and pimples; unclothed walkers develop a graceful style of walking. There is nothing miraculous here, it is just that we all have some talent for 'looking good'; either it is expressed through choice of clothing, hairstyles and so on, or else the unadorned body takes on the task itself and produces a similar effect. Tear the clothes off a dandy and he will look awkward, naked and absurd; whereas someone used to living in the minimum of clothing will look fully dressed beside him. Mr. Universe in swimming trunks looks fully clothed, but in clothes he looks clumsy and ungainly.

Reconstructions of the ancestors of homo sapiens do not show great beauty of form. In physical terms the beautiful savage is not our ancestor but our future model: for the white races with their thin lips and body hair are closer to the apes than the more physically evolved negro races.

Although, at the present, man does his best to hide and

THE BIG MEAT

ignore the human body, so it is not seen to great advantage; nevertheless in terms of real potential we must be growing more beautiful. Some writers have convinced themselves of half of this truth, believing that women have developed nice hair, soft skins and voluptuous breasts in order to please men. But what of the other half of the story? Has not the male human evolved to exaggerate his physical characteristics? Muscle is the adornment, or clothing, of the male body, so surely men must grow more muscular?

Again popular ideas oppose this. There is seen to be too strong a link between muscularity and strength; so the fact that the man of the future will not <u>need</u> strength means that he will not <u>need</u> muscle. Hence the idea that we will evolve into mekons. But, in an evolutionary timescale, intelligence will be made redundant just as quickly as strength. What matters is not the strength of muscle but its decorative quality. Present day body builders are much more muscular than even the Greek Gods. In general no animal has such prominent muscles as man. Gorillas look portly by comparison; and those exceptions (like horses) who match man are also amongst the most highly evolved creatures.

In the vast, airconditioned cities of the future, clothing will not be a necessity. If nature no longer exists in the form of wild life, she will express herself through human flesh. The revulsion that some people express at the idea of a Mr. Universe is seen to be awe in their actual physical presence, in the same way that an extreme extravert can be overwhelming. The future induces awe because it points out that we are the past.

I have scaled the mountain! An overpopulated world has been transformed from one long rush hour into a vista of gorgeous copulating human flesh, from a nightmare into a wanking phantasy. Glory Hallelujah - I am free!

(Lea's lengthy digression on Body Building as an Analogy of the Austin Spare Magical System and Alchemical Transmutation was edited out, for it really belongs in a separate treatise.)

One needs to have an army of defenses against obsessions,

beliefs, theories or Gods. We have seen how they can die of neglect, and how they can be frightened by direct challenge. Here we see another approach, analogous to mountain climbing.

It depends upon finding a weak point: a place for a foot hold. This depends upon aesthetic judgement - you play around the nightmare to find some point where fascination dominates revulsion.

The process of climbing is the method of degenerate science - of the sort that sells best selling books.

The danger of these best selling books is that one only reads the ones that tickle your own beliefs, ie. your obsessions choose the titles rather than yourself. For example the rationalist who reads books which claim to explode some myth, like the Bermuda Triangle, without reading the books which support the myth, or attack the 'exploder': People who read John Allegro without reading his critics: feminists who avoid allegedly 'sexist' works. A book which criticises Von Danniken is likely to quote him so much, that the reader feels it unnecessary to read the original; this is one reason why we succumb to the arguments of the second book.

Instead one should make a habit of reading both sides of such debates until you really understand how adaptable is the popular scientific approach: it allows one to present a convincing case for anything. Either certain facts fit your theory, in which case they are acceptable, or else they do not. If they do not there must be an explanation why they don't fit, why they are exceptions. If you cannot find such an explanation it means that there is not enough information. Therefore the facts can be dismissed as 'insufficiently well documented'.

Using this method one should be able to find the good side of any depressing thought.

The good side of a demon is always the back side.

17

MICROCOSMOS

These are viruses, and their cell-structure is incomplete so that
they are only fully operative when they become part of other cells.
In their own language, you may remember, they are called Experts.

Observe if you will, Ladies and Gentlemen, the operative cycle of an
Expert. You will see one of them entering a normal, differentiated
cell. Observe that it goes straight to the nucleus. It has the power
to do this because it is incomplete, and when it gets to the nucleus
it starts to rearrange the structure there. Remember, Ladies and
Gentlemen, the well-known law that only what is partial can change
what is complete. Your physicists split the atom, you may
remember, by bombarding it with parts of atoms, because whole
atoms leave it unchanged.

Observe how, shortly after the entry of the Expert, the normal
cell becomes larger and squarer, less like its neighbours, and
starts to multiply very rapidly into what are called (down there)
production plants and office blocks. You will also notice that many
of these large square cells break down and, instead of the one
Expert that went in, they release hundreds of new Experts, all
identically constructed, which rapidly disperse to infect more cells.
JAMES KEYS - ONLY TWO CAN PLAY THIS GAME

O H Leazus, my old DaddyJesus, you do like to go on about
evolution. It reminds me of a vision that I had.
Crump! My head expanded out to the stars, it seemed
as though I was falling inward, inward, inward. After some

66

MICROCOSMOS

unknown time I was in a jostling crowd of strange creatures, like
trembling blobs.

Curiously I could read their quivering skin language and
found that they were discussing evolution. Like you they could see
how they were progressing, growing into larger more complicated
and skillful blobs.

Disorientated at first, I grew accustomed to this world once
I felt that I understood it. I was able to take the shape of the other
blobs and so was able to speak their language.

"Fellow cells," I cried, "do I hear you discussing evolution?
Let me tell you that you have already evolved on a scale quite
beyond your wildest imagining! All together you form a society
called the Brain, you are brain cells. Together with all the other
forms of cell around you, you form a mighty body which lies
beyond your comprehension; yet every one of you contains within
you the blueprint of that macrocosm."

They called me a loony prophet; asked me how I knew this
was true. I explained that I knew because I was that greater body:
that I was God made cell. It seemed a good line and it won me
quite a following. I reminded them that I was encapsulated in them
(in the DNA code) just as they were in me; and that whosoever
clobbered his neighbour clobbered me. Yet somehow I bungled it;
and eventually they crucified me.

Just as it really got to hurt, the same thing happened all
over again! Crump! And I was shrinking once more.

What had once looked like cells, were now looking like
vast city states, and I was locked out. When I hammered on the
city gates powerful guards came out and pushed me away, despite
my pleading. In my despair I was almost tempted to try again to
pull the God bit on them, but instead I watched and waited.

I soon learnt that only the most noxious smoothies ever got
into this city. Anyone who was nice and easy-going was chucked
out; but anyone with a good line in bullshit seemed to overawe the
guards. But they did need papers.

Seeing a likely-looking candidate making his way to the gates,
I mugged him and pinched his papers. The papers stated that he was
a Doctor of Economics.

MICROCOSMOS

Now I knew very little about economics, but the guards were easily taken in. They were most polite when I flashed the papers before them; asked me what my business was in the city. With my heart in my mouth I gulped and said, in as cool a voice as I could muster, that I wished to implement a new marketing strategy based on a cost analysis that gave positive weighting to the income elasticity of demand. The guard looked uneasy and hastily agreed with me. "About time too, sir, if you don't mind me saying so," and he hurriedly waved me through.

It seemed to work. There were setbacks: like the times when my utterances made unintentional sense and lent themselves to being questioned. But overall I had found the secret of success. Everywhere I went doors were opened. I was promoted, under the repeated slogan of 'Market Maximisation' until I found myself on the board of some great financial empire.

It was a nice life, the other board members were so delightfully human. They could talk for hours about principles and ideals, but once I started my bullshit, one by one they fell silent. When I spoke of accelerated market dynamics one of them would desperately protest that it was 'not quite cricket' and I would squash him with "it may not be cricket, but what about the $11\frac{1}{2}$ per cent growth index parameter?" It was the numbers that did it: 'human' values seemed so vague alongside 'actual' figures, that one only had to lob in a few arbitrary numbers to silence opposition.

Shorn of vague and woolly concepts, management developed a hard efficiency: my nonsense utterances were like the mantram that silence the noise of the mind in meditation. Our empire grew with accelerating frenzy. Our city flourished beyond all others. It grew and grew and grew and grew, new cities sprang up all around, and the opposition crumbled to our takeovers.

And I woke in agony in a cancer ward of a hospital.

I leapt from my bed screaming "Why did I do it?". I rushed in search of tablet bottles, anything that would be fatal in overdose, crying,"The end of your world is nigh, for I, the Lord your God hath cocked it up!"

The nurses fell upon me and I felt the needle's jab. "It's pressing on his brain," one said and I awoke again in my own bed nuzzling the tumbling red hair of my sleeping girl, whose tender arms were enfolded with mine.

Verily I had been saved from a socialist devil dream. If specialisation is a carcinogen what is the status of the free spirit in the body of mankind? Are viruses responsible for the good changes as well as the bad in our lives? Is the health of a society dependent upon its strength to resist us as well as its failure to exterminate us?

18

THE ECOGNOMICS OF UNCLEAR POWER

Progress should be closely examined and what you have gained
by the convenience of science
                    AUSTIN SPARE - THE BOOK OF PLEASURE
a witch is a rebel in physics and a rebel is a witch in politics
                    THOMAS VAUGHAN - ANTHROPOSOPHIA THEOMAGICA

IN its own world Economics has, apparently, performed miracles; and yet it has a very poor record as it impinges on _my_ reality. Every week the New Scientist and such popular technology papers give accounts of new techniques in manufacture which promise to economise on materials, energy and labour; but how often do we see retail prices dropping as a result?

I recall that artificial leather for shoes was to lead to a new age of cheaper footwear. Instead the new shoes have come in at the price of leather shoes, and the latter have moved up to a luxury price range.

The popular resistance to continental-sized container lorries in Britain was eroded with the message that the lorries would economise on transport costs, and yet prices have increased since their arrival. The retort is usually to suggest that prices would have increased by even more without them, but I remain cynical. I very much suspect that in this case, as in any other case where pure economics has been use to defeat human instincts and aesthetic judgements, that if one were to draw graphs of the increase in retail prices and the increased use of large lorries, then there would be a strong correlation. Another example is Tankard ale; here the arguments for it were economically so strong: it kept better, it did not need

expert handling and anyone could serve it; it also travelled better
so it could be brewed centrally. But here again I suspect that the
higher price of beer correlates closely with the rise of tankard ale.

Why is this? We do not like big lorries - why? One only
has to stand in a narrow High Street trying to shout over them, or
to be stuck behind one in a traffic jam, to realise that one does not
like them. The question "why?" is just a waste of time because the
answer is an infinite chain of aesthetic objections. So when some
goon stands before us with some (probably false) figures about the
saving in taxpayer's money made by the lorries, then all the
objections seem trifling in comparison. Considered as a battle,
it is like setting a tank against a crowd of a myriad unarmed
people.

But what happens in such a battle? The people will win
once they learn to run away. With time the tank will run out of
fuel, grow rusty, break down, while the people go on breeding and
surviving.

So it is with those myriad little objections to huge lorries.
The objections are still there, despite the economic argument; and
they can quietly defeat the economic argument. One saving is that
two small lorries require two drivers whilst one large one requires
only one. A halving of costs? Perhaps. But will the driver of the
larger lorry not suffer from the greater responsibility, the greater
public resistance to his vehicle and other difficulties such as
parking and loss of flexibility; and will it not make him want a
higher wage? And can you really halve your workforce without
expensive resistance? And how can one evaluate the cost of
larger lorries to the population who have to put up with them?

When economics fails in such ways, it is tempting to look
at each individual element of the defeat in terms of economics; and
to argue that what is therefore needed is more economics, new
techniques to allow for all these factors. But in SSOTBME it was
suggested that any events in real life are linked by an infinite series
of ever-diminishing causes, and that the method of any science with
its basis on logic must be to cut the series at some point and to
consider all later terms as negligible. But it was pointed out also
that the insignificance of causative links is relative: eliminate, or

deal with, the large links and the small ones will then become the dominant factors, because they are beyond the field of prediction (as when major diseases are wiped out, with the result that the population increases and becomes prey to diseases which were previously ignorable).

So, as long as economics at least pretends to be a science, it will never really have any way of matching the aesthetic judgement which might have spared us the juggernaut. So why not forget economics in such cases and listen to the humans?

"Ah, but if we did that we would never even have built the railways!"

"But in view of the huge subsidies you tell us are needed in order to maintain a lousy service, is not the original human rejection proved right?"

If you get a job in an economics research group (go on, do it!) and you maintain a secret cynical eye, you will feel a little like a rationalist at an evangelical rave-up. You will witness the creation of economic myth, and become a wiser magician.

I recall seeing in an economic journal the sentence 'there is no doubt about it, the High Street store is dead'; and it went on to criticise such stores for their '19th Century inefficiency'. And to think economics is meant to be a science! If I judge that remark in terms of my own reality it is ludicrous: how can the High Street store be dead while they still exist and are open six days a week? What is meant by 'inefficiency'? In the 19th Century a small sweet shop, or a farm of just a few acres, was capable of supporting a family. If this is no longer true, then one could argue that we are now, in a sense, able to make _less_ efficient use of the land. Food mountains which never reach _us_ at low prices, are no signs of efficiency in _my_ reality. Indeed it is hard to evade the conclusion that economics and the pursuit of 'efficiency' is a very costly parasite on mankind.

By saying that the High Street store was dead, those economists were giving birth to their reality by _believing_ it. By repeating such formulae they make them come true: investment in High Street stores will eventually decrease, and aspiring young career men will sense the wind and divert their

energies elsewhere. If the High Street store does die in the name
of economics, it will be by magic and not by science.

In the hard light of experience economics seems to fade like
a demon of the night; but surely nuclear power is not of the same
order, being a physical reality rather than a concept? But look
again, how do we know it is real?

I recall the pre-war newspaper announcement of the first
experiments in splitting the atom. It was reported that there were
two possible outcomes: heaven or doomsday. Either we would live
to see an age of unlimited cheap power, or else a chain reaction
could be started which would destroy the whole universe. Certainly
the first has not taken place; I have sometimes considered the
possibility that the second did actually take place. But let us be
really daring! Wild anarchists that we are, let us show two
fingers to the brain police and dare to suggest that there is a third
possibility: namely that the nuclear physicists were talking bullshit.

Do you accept second-hand accounts of Uri Geller's powers?
He is not claiming very great ability compared with some people who
claim that they can destroy a city with one small bomb: have you
ever seen them do it? When we are taught to be suspicious of
spiritualists who insist on working in the dark, what are we to make
of nuclear physicists who do not ever allow any observers within a
hundred miles of their tests?

I am so privileged in this respect, I have seen an atomic
pile. But it was the most pathetic piece of evidence imaginable.
There was a green glow at the bottom of a tank of water, and
information to be read on dials. Anybody could stick a light bulb
at the bottom of a tank. When I considered diving in to see if my
hair fell out, or I got diarrhoea, or any such effects, I was of
course forbidden, 'for my own safety'. It would have been like
taking a torch into a spiritualist's seance.

Uri Geller sets out to demonstrate something, and he does
it in my presence. In reply the scientists make absurd suggestions
that he has radio sets in his teeth, or some other phantasy.

Nuclear physicists extract millions of pounds from the
government (for which I thank them) to do something that they refuse

to demonstrate. Even among scientists themselves there are doubts as to the practicality of nuclear energy, so what am I supposed to believe? Above all should I allow myself to live in the shadow of other people's invisible devils? Is this not another obsession which will go away if ignored?

What would a community of non-scientists make of the theory of nuclear energy? What if we returned to a 'primitive' feudal society and archaeologists of the distant future came across a book about nuclear energy, how would it be received?

Perhaps we should ask how we receive the findings of archaeologists? If an Essene scripture, an alchemical or magical manuscript, or a text about spiritual enlightenment is found, what happens to it nowadays?

Let us imagine an alchemical manuscript that tells us how to achieve our hearts' desires. It outlines some mysterious processes in strange terminology; it tells us that explanation is not enough and that a lifetime of dedicated seeking and a whole-hearted trust in God is necessary. But it insists that, given these factors, we cannot fail. Let us ask what the official reaction to such a find would be. Does a university or government research body advertise for someone who believes in God and is prepared to dedicate a lifetime in alchemic quest, in order to test the worth of the manuscript?

The answer is no. Although society is now so rich in money that we are prepared to risk millions on a nuclear gamble, we are in fact so poor in time and trust that nobody is officially prepared to dedicate a lifetime to test an alchemical theory. (Unofficial testers are therefore suspicious and their conclusions therefore annulled.)

Similarly with our chieftain of the future, whose archaeologists have found a nuclear physics text: it is unlikely that he will be rich enough in money to set up the industries and the mining and refining operations, in order to put to the test this Book of Power; though he might well be in a position to find a hermit prepared to put the above mentioned alchemical processes to the test. So what does he make of 'the Book'?

Well, what do we make of alchemy? Because its application makes huge demands upon time and upon faith - both in short supply

THE ECONOMICS OF UNCLEAR POWER

at present - it is not considered to be 'real'. So it is viewed
symbolically: it is seen in terms of psychology, or religion. It
is not officially believed that anyone ever could make gold, but
that the text is a primitive attempt to symbolise various inner
processes, or religious beliefs.

Perhaps the future will see nuclear physics in these terms.
Because its application makes huge demands upon money and
resources, which may well be in short supply, perhaps it will not
be considered as real, but merely symbolic.

One of Lemuel Johnstone's hobbies was inventing such
symbolic interpretations of our present dominant beliefs as a
gift for future ages: so that they might be liberated from the
inconvenience of literal belief, just as we are now liberated
from literal belief in the ideas of past ages.

Considering the splitting of the atom, he would ask if the
family could be seen as the atom of society. If the family could be
divided against itself, then its collapse could start a chain reaction
that would explode society. Or if the individual was the atom in a
group, then an individual divided against himself would start the
reaction.

Density of population was essential for this effect, there
was a Critical Mass which was approached in large cities,
scattered village communities could not explode in isolation.
Heavy atoms, ie. large families, were most effective. The initial
splitting could either take place spontaneously when the population
reached the Critical Mass, or else it could be initiated by injecting
such ideas as the 'generation gap', or ideological differences.
They should be injected at high energy levels, having been accelerated
down a media channel where a series of magnetic personalities gave
momentum to the ideas.

The collapse of society releases a surge of energy, quite out
of proportion to its normal effective energy. The object is to try,
as Hitler did, to control and direct the energy, or else simply to
explode the old order in order to destroy surrounding cultures
with the resulting fall-out.

Another of Johnstone's theories was the Theory of General
Psychic Relativity. As it was our beliefs that so obviously shaped

our reality, why was it so difficult to make huge changes in reality with a simple shifting of belief? What was it that gave beliefs their inertia, or 'mass'?

He decided that the inertia of a belief was not a property inherent in itself, but that it was a function of all the other minds in its universe, ie. all the other minds that held that belief.

For this reason the biggest magic tended to take place in isolated groups, or else demanded that one lived a period in isolation as a hermit. To turn stones into bread in the wilderness was one thing, the inertia overcome was the inertia generated by one mind. But to turn stones into bread before a sceptical crowd, although at first sight no bigger a task, in fact required one to overcome the inertia of a much larger universe.

Various other deductions followed which could be verified, eg. the light of truth tended to be deflected from its course by massive populations and so on. But the most interesting idea was the challenge it presented to one's desire to astound a materialist world. Don't we anarchists long to shatter scientific smugness with the ultimate in irrefutable evidence for magic? But to do so would, in the terms of our present age, be the ultimate in evil. The materialist viewpoint is the foundation of our age, it is the God of our day. To shatter that would be no small thing, however 'small' the evidence you produced. From the point of view of the spirit of our age you would be the Antichrist itself, responsible for the destruction of a world.

19

DOWN WITH REALITY

In dreams, writes Coleridge, images represent the sensations we
think they cause: we do not feel horror because we are threatened
by a sphinx; we dream of a sphinx in order to explain the horror we
feel.

J. L. BORGES - DREAMTIGERS

"What you have done is no triumph," he said. "You've wasted a
beautiful power, a power that blew life into that dry twig .... It
doesn't matter .... that branch was a real animal and it was
alive at the moment the power touched it. Since what kept it alive
was power, the trick was like in <u>dreaming</u>, to sustain the sight of
it. See what I mean?"

CARLOS CASTANEDA - JOURNEY TO IXTLAN

AT the beginning we quoted Simon who could see no value
in offering resistance to any government because, contrary
to their own belief, governers are powerless. What
politician has affected our lives as much as the Beatles have? Yet
the Beatles set out to make music, not to change the tastes of the
Western World. It is not people that rule us, but fashions, beliefs,
demons and gods. It was against such tyrants that we have fought.

If you have kept with us you will have gained some skill at
the guerilla warfare for the mind, you will see how bullying fears
can be surmounted, disected, or scared away. Without them one
returns to reality, to freedom. But are we free? Can you fly?
or move mountains?

No, because this cannot happen in reality.

Whose reality? We have grown so used to seeing through

77

other people's visions of our world, should we not extend our cynicism towards reality itself?

It was argued in the last chapter that any utterly irrefutable evidence of some paranormal phenomena would destroy our world, because we live in a materialist world. In SSOTBME it was explained that, contrary to many people's hopes, the materialist world cannot be stretched to allow just a little magic, because the world is not flexible. It is brittle, and would shatter rather than stretch to make room for magic.

The basis of materialism is logical thought which gives rise to hard and brittle theories, and shapes a hard and brittle world. It is a world of Utter Certainty, and we foolishly want a little magic to enter the world of Utter Certainty.

The anarchist in me is beginning to hate this world of Utter Certainty! So let us look at it - that always scares a ruler who would rather see lowered eyes than a direct gaze.

Once I saw a ghost; this particular ghost was remembered for the lesson it taught me. I felt shock and sat up in my bed to see a man with a dagger raised and his hideous face contorted with rage as he leaned over my bed. In terror I froze, and felt my scalp prickling with fear.

In my waking state I realised that what I was seeing was impossible - 'it could not be'. I stared harder, blinking my eyes and telling myself that it could not be.

Sure enough, the figure melted into the light and shade patterns of a crumpled curtain at the end of the bed. I had explained away the apparition: it was an optical illusion.

But it had been so alarming that I remained unmoving and I continued to stare. If it was an optical illusion I should be able to see the face still, if I tried to make it reappear. But I could not do it. There was an unsymmetrical situation here: the face had clearly faded into the curtain, but I could not now see how the curtain could look like a face.

To an unsceptical materialist this might not seem surprising: he would understand that reality was like solid ground, I had dropped into reality and that was where I should stay. But this 'moral' view was unsatisfying to me, because most other optical illusions that

DOWN WITH REALITY

I've seen continue to amuse the eye even after they have been explained. To me this 'reality' was not simply exerting a gravitational pull that made it difficult for me to reform my illusion; it was more like a prison whose gates had shut behind me.

Instead I chose the magical explanation, for it seemed less bizarre. The magical explanation was that I had banished the ghost.

How had I done it? By staring hard, blinking my eyes and thinking 'this cannot be so'. This hard concentrated stare corresponds to the tarot suit of swords, and the sword is the magician's prime weapon of banishment. Remember this technique if ever you are alone in a haunted house; the courage to do it comes from the knowledge (belief?) that it works.

Now what happens when a sceptical scientist is present at a demonstration of paranormal powers? Almost certainly he will, stare hard, blink his eyes and think 'this cannot be'. Confident in his belief, he will banish the magic.

This is the basic fallacy built into all scientific investigation of magical or 'paranormal' phenomena. For an account of its effect see Lyall Watson's books Supernature and The Romeo Error. He gives examples such as the Loch Ness Monster surveying team who spent weeks searching with all their scientific apparatus and yet only saw the monster once, on one morning when their apparatus was not ready to hand. What they saw was personally convincing, yet was utterly worthless as evidence without their scientific recording techniques. Why, he asks, is it that paranormal phenomena only seem to appear when our guards are down, and we are unprepared for them? Why do they not re-appear in the laboratory conditions?

Surely the magician can answer this query: laboratory conditions are themselves a banishing ritual within a magic circle, and they are designed to banish all that is inimical to scientific work; therefore they banish the paranormal.

MacGregor Mathers points out an unusual feature in the Abra Melin system in his introduction to the handbook: there is no physica magic circle in the system. But he points out that the six months of discipline have had an equivalent effect of purifying and banishing unwelcome elements from the oratory and sleeping quarters -- the circle exists in an intangible form. So it is with the laboratory: a place kept clean and ordered, the donning of white lab. coats, the exclusion of distracting emotional, financial or personal considerations during one's work, are all elements more or less present and consistently reinforcing the sanctity of the area. As in the Abra Melin work this sanctity will infuse the whole life of the dedicated scientist and he will never suffer the torments of the paranormal.

So if Uri Geller is to bend a spoon to the complete satisfaction of the scientific community, it will be a double miracle: one is the very small miracle of bending a spoon, the other is the enormous yet unrecognised miracle of defeating the most powerful banishing ritual in the world today.

To the anarchist the idea of challenging that power is attractive; but I feel that it is unlikely to be defeated by head-on confrontation, but rather by guerilla tactics. It will be necessary to undermine the firm belief that supports the system. The resulting victory will of course, as in all victories, be an illusion. If we do manage to create a new Science that admits magic to its laboratories it will only be Science by name: the old dogmatism will have been banished but not destroyed. We will be deprived of the pleasure of seeing today's rationalists crying their eyes out. This is in itself a good thing, because that very pleasure is as much a snare as the god we wish to banish.

Earlier we referred to the materialist's state of Utter Certainty, where truth was hard and brittle. I recall Jonathan Miller on a BBC discussion programme rejecting astrology's claims to be a science because its conclusions did not have that 'brittle' quality he expected of a science. The above mentioned banishing technique is the police force of that State of Utter Certainty. The first thing to do is to recognise it for what it is - namely a banishing ritual - and already the State has lost some of its mystique.

Next we realise that this police force is open to corruption, it can be bought. This is of course what was done in the last

DOWN WITH REALITY

chapter. Economics was given the test of Utter Certainty and it
vanished. We did not ask it to prove itself in the laboratory, but
rather in our own subjectively conceived lives. In that world no
amount of economic argument could destroy the one clear
observation that economics was an expensive delusion. This
technique has been recommended throughout this book: if you take
any political or moral theory and subject it to the same sort of
rigorous analysis that a scientist would give to a haunted house
then you come to the same conclusion: the ghost is an illusion.

This banishment is the strength of science as of any other
magic. It is also the liberating force of the right wing anarchist
up to the point that he must recognise it for what it is - merely a
banishment. If he forgets that fact, he has merely bowed down
before a new tyrant – Utter Certainty.

But the later part of the last chapter was a bit more
remarkable: it is one thing to banish a woolly pseudo-science like
economics, but can one really banish nuclear power which is itself
the product of pure science?

To this extent one can. What is the use of an Utter Certainty
in a laboratory to which we are denied access? So if instead we
apply the test to our own subjective lives and find that atomic power
only exists therein as a metaphor, then we are justified in refusing
to be further bothered by it.

The Utter Certainty Test has been so developed and
strengthened by science that it is in danger of being turned on science
itself and has been in such books as Kuhn's 'Structure of Scientific
Revolutions'. All such philosophical arguments can only be effective
on fertile ground, the same being true of real life experience, but
all the same there is nothing like scientific work for liberating one
from delusion.

Now I know you have already been asked to become a Civil
Servant, a policeman, a teacher and an economic researcher; but
if you are an anarchist you must expect an exciting life.

So if you join a high technology team, and do not allow
yourself to be carried away by the dream, you will learn the same
lesson as you did as an 'economist'. To the outside world there is
a facade of hard facts and logic, any attack on that facade being

defended by the Utter Certainty banishing test. But behind that
facade you will find a very familiar hotch potch of personalities,
emotional judgements, bungling, confusion and poor communication.
The harder you search for Real Science, the more elusive it will be.
You will be forced to realise that nuclear technology is not really
the outcome of a rigid system called 'physics', but rather simply
something that happens. Whether it happens in the name of
christianity, science or magic is almost irrelevant, for it simply
happens. Each factor which could be expected to reinforce the
rigid scientific basis is just as likely to endanger it in practice:
for example the introduction of computers results in such an
indigestible mass of information that the receiver of this information is forced to resort to feeling judgements when it comes to
making use of the results. We find the same snag that bedevilled
the thought police in chapter 13: an incomplete model is powerful
but unrealistic, as the model tends towards completeness it tends
towards a reproduction, or restatement, of the original problem,
rather than towards a solution.

Most amazing of all is that you will find evidence of magic
at work: experiments that only work because of the experimenter's
own strong belief and so on. This would seem to belie the
banishing nature of the scientific method, until you realise that it
is the scientific method that is absent. Indeed it is tempting to
outrage decency by suggesting that the parascience laboratories
are the last bastions of the true scientific method, for they are
the only laboratories where doubt still reigns over wish fulfill-
ment.

So let us look back at this stage.

We began by observing the extent to which people are not
free, but are tyrannised by their obsessions. Gradually we learn
to overthrow the tyrants and regain our freedom. But as we
approach the state of ultimate freedom bitterness sets in. We
have destroyed so much that we are lonely in a desert. Without
the adrenalin kicks of political and religious frenzy we are cool
and bored. All is reduced to the desert of Utter Certainty. Free
from the distinctions of delusion we are faced with our true
impotence. There is only the Real World and the Laws of Nature

against which we are powerless.

At this stage there are two choices; how shall we describe
them? The way of the magician versus the way of the mystic?
perhaps more truly the way of low magic versus the way of high
magic? Even the way of sorcery against the way of true magic?
All these pairs of terms reflect the distinction we shall make.

The first way is to deliberately repopulate the desert
oneself, to create your own world under your own dominion, to
choose your own beliefs and let them work for you.

The second way is to recognise that all the destruction of
tyranny so far completed was merely a preparation, a lopping of
the bureaucracy, and the real tyrant behind it all still remains.
The real tyrant is the desert itself, it is one's view of reality.
So the completion of the task is to break through this last barrier.

It is the latter way which is considered to be the 'higher'
way, and we find this parallel in many magical systems. Crowley
calls the magicians 'black' who choose not to eliminate the last
vestiges of their 'ego' but rather to turn back and play power games
with demons. Certainly it is dangerous to believe that you can
set up your own kingdom on earth and not fall slowly under the
power of your own creation so long as you have failed to destroy
the ultimate tyrant.

The sadness that makes one want to turn back is the
Dweller on the Threshold of this Abyss. One has weaned oneself
off the opiates of mass movements and mob fancies and now feels
lonely. One has forgotten the price of pain and now sees only the
fun. Nostalgie de la boue draws one back and one is haunted by a
sense of lost innocence.

All this nastiness is reason enough to advocate the last
assault as the only true solution, but it is in fact so difficult that
other things must be considered first. This is partly to consolidate
our position but also as an insurance: lest even the sense of 'higher
truth' should itself be delusion we must at least explore the low
magic at this stage.

So let us take a few paces backwards before the final assault.

20

MAPS AND SORCERY

"Hark how the little birds sing of love," sang the little old lady on
the park bench.

"That's aggression, not love! They're staking a territorial claim
when they make that noise," sneered the acne-scarred youth by her
side.

Why did he say that? Was the fleeting intellectual triumph really
worth the effort? See! how quickly the old dear has forgotten his
remark and returned to blissful contemplation. But does he look
any happier for his knowledge?

They live in two quite different models of reality. Society would
call him 'strong minded'. But he bears his reality like an
irritating burden, whereas she has disciplined the world into a
cornucopia of joy. Should we not then admit that, though not so
strong in mind, she is at least the stronger in soul?

FROM AN UNPUBLISHED DRAFT OF S.S.O.T.B.M.E.

WHAT happens when we are moved by a good lecture, or
a good non-fiction book? As we come away from, say, an
interesting lecture on psychology, we are for a short while
living in a different reality: the world is the world of that psychology
lecture. But it is more acceptable if we rephrase this and say that
we are temporarily living with a different 'map' of the world. A
competant lecturer, who avoids actual confrontation with the ideas
of his audience, is like someone who lays out a new map of part
of the world and points out features on that map.

We live our lives on mental maps and so it is easy to forget
this fact. Most obviously we have actual geographical maps, and
we forget they are personal to us. For example we meet someone

from Singapore and we ask if they know our friends the Tresizes.
They laugh and remind us that Singapore is a large place; we blush,
for we realise that in <u>reality</u> it is, but we had been forgetfully
referring to our own mental map of the world.

Yet we happily jump from map to map: as we plan a walking
trip in the Pennines we have the physical map of Britain in mind
with its hills and woods. As we plan the journey to the Pennines
we transfer to a road map view of Britain, and perhaps even a
train or bus-route map. Crossing London we have an A to Z
type of street map view, but also an underground map picture of
the capital.

But the endpapers of the New Anatomy of Britain show a
very different map of Britain, one which shows the relationship
between the various sociological and political divisions of the
country. The signs of the zodiac are a map of the world: they are
not just twelve isolated boxes, but stand in definite relationships
to each other.

We can happily jump from map to map and yet forget that
we are dealing with maps, and this can cause trouble. For if the
zodiac really is a description of all people surely it is reasonable
to ask which signs are introvert and which are extravert? One
can in fact line up 'positive' and 'negative' signs with 'extravert'
and 'introvert', but the match is not exact. It is a bit like trying
to line up the underground map with a street map of London.
Worse still, one could ask which signs are Labour, which are
Liberal and which Tory? That is like trying to line up the Anatomy
of Britain map with a geographical map. So people who seek to
test astrology by giving someone's birth date and asking the astro-
loger to determine if the person was born into the aristocracy, are
in fact confusing maps.

But even if we remember that we are living on maps, we
still are not all-powerful. One thing I find difficult is to make a
firm link between the astronomical map of the universe, and my
own maps of the world. On a starry night stand outside, think
of the world as you know it stretching all around, and then think
of the stars and planets as other worlds. Now try to link the two
so that you feel the earth beneath you really is just another planet

85

like those distant points of light. It is an interesting meditation.

We are in fact all to some extent at the mercy of our maps.
When Angerford had a spell on the dole, he used to explain to his
relatives that in view of the atrocious state of the country under
Labour rule, he did not feel he could continue to be a taxpayer
with a good conscience. He said this because his relatives lived
on a particular world map on which people who lived on the dole
were all lazy, left wing scroungers. So, by adopting a stance
that was difficult to align with that map, he silenced further
criticism.

Our view of the world is coloured and distorted by the maps
we use. This is not just a question of opinion being distorted, but
even observation itself. Kuhn describes in 'The Structure of
Scientific Revolutions' (p.63) an experiment where people were
asked to identify playing cards rapidly flashed on a screen. But
some of the cards were 'paranormal', eg. a red six of spades or
black ace of hearts. At speed these were not seen as miracles,
but were named as actual cards. Even at longer exposures, the
viewers still did not recognise these paranormal cards for what
they were. Because their mental map only included the fifty-two
normal cards, their minds made what they saw fit on that map.
But when given an even longer exposure (up to forty times that
required to identify normal cards), the delusion began to break
down. Even now they were not quick to see what was wrong, but
tended to feel a bit uncomfortable and say 'something was funny',
without yet knowing what it was. But when the trick was explained,
the cards were recognised for what they were.

This simple example clearly shows the mechanism by
which the materialist fails to notice or recognise the paranormal
in his life, because it does not exist on his world map. Similarly
the furious anti-semite cannot see the kindness of his Jewish
neighbours, the rabid Tory cannot see Labour's successful
economic measures, and so on. If we live on restricted maps we
live a restricted life.

So we seek to get back from maps to reality, and we realise
that reality itself could be another map. Being born into a world
where materialist philosophy has been king for at least a century,

it is almost certain that a materialist world-view is the basis for that map called 'reality'.

We have re-traced our steps. Being dominated by a demon is to be trapped on a particular map. An over-simple map is an instrument of power, but also a trap for its user: persuade a people that there is a simple division into Good and Bad and you can apparently rule them; but you are in fact just the mouthpiece for the idea, which is the true ruler.

It is beginning to seem possible that the 'brittle' quality of the materialist map of reality is not a quality related to materialism itself, it is simply the quality of dessication and fossilisation of an old map which has been hanging up too long. To the devout churchman of the past, the Christian map would have had the same sharp brittle quality, and the new scientific ideas would have seemed like woolly delusion.

Now let us turn back to sorcery.

A sorcerer is someone who conjures his own demons, or chooses his own maps to suit his own desires. When faced with an insoluble dilemma he will not be daunted by belief of man's finite capacity, but will opt to believe in the tarot, astrology, I Ching or whatever system is available, and will accept its advice without fear. In practical work he will be happy to use whatever means are available to bring about changes in accordance with his will; apart from all the normal techniques he will feel free to use the paranormal techniques of magic.

Having discovered how people are imprisoned by their beliefs (so that the materialist viewpoint can only permit one to witness materialist phenomena), he will choose to believe in whatever system that will allow the effect he wants to take place. In other words he will choose a map that includes that possibility.

Maps are descriptions of the world, so they are of the same order of reality as language itself. Within a map we work in a systematic one-dimensional manner, that is to say we use logical thought to work on a map. One of the commonest misunderstandings about logic is for people to deny logic to others who are using it correctly, but on a different map to their own. But outside of maps

there is no structure on which to base our logic. So the thought
process which enables one to jump from map to map is not logic,
but something more akin to aesthetic judgement. I associate it
with the idea of 'feeling', as described in SSOTBME.

To deny that there is any thought process but logic, good
or bad, is to deny the existence of feeling and to deny the possibility of sorcery. And unless we are prepared to go beyond the
limits of language and logic we will remain prisoners on one map.

A thorough investigation of this sorcery inevitably leads
us back to the question of the high magic, because, in this case,
we are likely to be disappointed by the results. We probably get
good results in divination, have a few runs of luck, but never really
learn to perform miracles.

What happens is that we are still dominated by our basic
notion of reality, and what is possible. It is as though that limit-
ation was always there at the back of our minds; as though we were
not so much swapping maps, but rather taking different maps and
laying them over our basic original map, so that it can still be
faintly seen. Real freedom to swap maps is difficult because some
maps are very heavy, they possess inertia on account of the
previously described principle of General Psychic Relativity. The
basic map of reality is too heavy to move.

The reason that divination has worked is that, even in a
materialist age, we do have an idea of a clever 'subconscious
mind' that can see things beyond our conscious ken, and this idea
allows us to get quite impressive results from divination. What is
more the amoral materialist world view does allow one to have
'lucky breaks' or 'coincidences', even though it does not allow you
to turn lead into gold. As a result we can make some predictions,
and improve our luck by magic, despite a basic materialist education.

So we still need to do some work on this ultimate tyranny;
and it is worth considering how people do survive under tyrannical
laws. One can either knuckle under, or one can be, to a small extent,
a lawbreaker, or one can manipulate the law to one's own advantage.

Being a lawbreaker can only be done on a small scale or else
it attracts attention, and you give yourself away with your own guilt.

MAPS AND SORCERY

The secret is to be just a bit carefree about the minor laws, then you won't cause much harm and will be let off lightly if caught.

What this means in our terms is that you <u>allow</u> more to happen, you do not feel obliged to 'explain it away'. Let us imagine that you open your wallet and find more money in it than you anticipated. The normal reaction is to seek an explanation, to think about it until you 'remember' that a friend repaid an old debt yesterday; then you feel satisfied. All your life you have done that, you reward your mind for finding explanations, you worry it until it does. Each time you reinforce your dependence on the materialist map.

In 'Journey to Ixtlan', Castaneda describes a ghost story which was similar in structure to the one described in the last chapter. In the desert twilight with Don Juan, he sees a horrible monster crouching. In terror he stares at it, forces himself to walk towards it, says 'it cannot be'. Sure enough, it melts into the play of light on an old dead branch; he has 'explained' it. He feels rather pleased with himself: he did not panic but kept his head and saw the monster for the illusion it 'really' was. But does Don Juan congratulate him? No, he tells him off for killing the magic. He accuses Castaneda not of seeing 'reality' but of forcing the world into his own idea of reality.

So instead of probing the past for an 'explanation' of the extra money just accept it with a non-explanation of this kind: 'the money has increased because I needed it'. If you see a ghost, call it a ghost, and do not force an explanation onto it. If you see a friend in a street when you know he is abroad then allow him to be in two places at once. If a book has moved to another room assume that it wanted to move and did so, rather than thinking back to when you 'unconsciously' picked it up, or a friend 'must have' taken it.

This is the way of thought of many present day witches: they do not set out to shatter the accepted world view, instead they quietly and in the nicest possible way, ignore some of its rules. They <u>allow</u> magic into their world.

This technique seems to be easier for the feminine mind, perhaps because society has trained women to be less in awe of authority, trained them in the art of smiling sweetly and getting away with murder; or perhaps there is some innate reason for this. The masculine mind often finds it easier to get round legal systems by studying them carefully to find legal loopholes. This was the technique used by Lemuel Johnstone when he found that the all-too-credible materialist world view was cramping his sense of adventure. He described it as a method of growing flowers in a desert.

His favourite starting point was the computer model of the brain, and the idea that the difference between the human mind and a simple computer was a difference in degree rather than quality. A sufficiently large computer would be expected to show all the attributes we expect from human thought: imagination, warmth, creativity, and so on.

When studied, this view is not one to be easily dismissed. In fact it is easily defended by a rather 'unfair' argument which depends on the limitations of language. If someone says, for example, that it is untrue 'because how could a computer develop a sense of beauty?' then you insist that their question is meaning-less unless they give a precise logical description of what is meant by 'a sense of beauty'. This is 'unfair' because to give a 'precise logical description' of anything is to put it into machine terms, ie. it is to give a description of how to make a machine that has that quality.

It is as though I insisted that God was an Englishman, he made the world in English, according to English instructions; all foreign languages are subsequent developments created by humans. Then you object, saying that if this was so how can the Chinese, for example, have developed concepts which lie beyond the scope of the English language - for example the 'Tao'. I say that is non-sense, I ask "what exactly do you mean by Tao, if anything?". Now if you do manage to explain it in English, then you have destroyed your own case by showing how Tao could be a development from the English language.

This means that the machine intelligence argument is a strong one, and is therefore credible, and is therefore a good basis for magic.

One idea that is useful in magic, but unacceptable to the

modern materialist, is the idea of a 'universal mind'. It is the
idea which allows us to say that plants grow on neglected buildings
because 'nature wants to reclaim her territory', that birds
developed wings because they 'wanted to' fly. Call the universe
God, and the desire to communicate with it is understandable.

The way in which Johnstone allowed the universal mind to
appear on the machine intelligence map of the world has been out-
lined in another book (SSOTBME) so will only be summarised
here. It consists of reversing the usual argument: 'there is no
purpose or will in simple mechanism, there is no qualitative
difference between simple mechanism and man, therefore there is
no purpose or will in man or anywhere in nature', and finding the
following argument: 'I detect purpose and will in my own thought,
I am told that there is no qualitative difference between myself and
simple mechanism, therefore the elements of purpose and will
exist even in simple mechanism'.

You see a computer need not be made of transistors and
wires. A free stone in space is a computer because it can
calculate (if several forces act upon it, then its subsequent motion
will reveal the resultant of those forces) and it has a memory
(because it will continue to move in a straight line in the direction
of that resultant, until a new force acts on it). Interacting streams
of fluid have been used as computers, in the form of fluidic control
systems. When a breeze sighs through a tree, the currents of air
seeping around the leaves and twigs form an immensely complex
system of interacting elements, of at least the same order of
complexity as your own brain. So should not this fleeting tree
spirit have thoughts as interesting as one's own? Is it really so
foolish to sit under the tree in contemplation of the sighing wind
and fluttering leaves, seeking to commune with the tree spirit?

The underground root structure which sends up the
psilocybe mushroom is as complex a network as the neural structure of a human brain. Is it really so fanciful to suggest that the
tiny mushrooms are given psychedelic properties as a deliberate
attempt to communicate with human or animal minds? Convince
yourself that all is rubbish, and it will be rubbish.

In SSOTBME there was also reference made to the way in
which the computer world supports the theory of reincarnation.

MAPS AND SORCERY

Johnstone went even further than this in 'Johnstone's 20th Century Occult Philosopher', and as that book was never published, I will summarise the relevant parable. It described the world when it had become hopelessly overpopulated: one huge edifice like a vast battery farm, and basic problems such as excess heat were endangering mankind. It was found that there was only one solution and that was to link all the computers into one super computer, and to programme everyone's mind into that computer, so that they could continue to live in the form of a computer dream, rather than in the form of physical reality. For if we only perceive the world via the brain, and the brain is a computer, then why do we need the world? Why not just live inside a computer and 'imagine' the world? So this was done. For political reasons explained in the story, the people were 'reborn' into a throwback world, a world modelled on the real world at the earliest moments of man's awakening consciousness. Many such parallel worlds were created to accomodate the excessive population. The tale ended with the scheme's founder coming round in the body of a tribal sage, and observing the world he had created. He realised that already children were being born in the new reality, for whom the past was but a myth. He realised that there was no chance of leaving a message for the future except by enshrining his knowledge in some huge megalithic stuctures. A 'descent of God' had been programmed into the future too. At this point it became clear that the story was perhaps set in the past, and that we were in fact the product of his work: we were living in that dream. Perhaps myths of giants and miracles were memories of the old reality; perhaps megaliths were built by people more knowledgable than us; perhaps there really are other parallel realities. Above all, this would mean that our laws of physics were arbitrary, and magic could be programmed into the world just as easily as science.

Again Johnstone had turned the normal argument upside down. Usually it is argued that if a machine universe can duplicate all the functions we used to ascribe to 'spirit' and 'soul', then we do not need those concepts and so, by Occam's Razor, should abandon them. Instead, Johnstone asked, 'why do we need all the complexities of the physical world? If all is explicable in terms of mind, then let us get rid of the physical world, and do a more thorough razor-job.' The fact that we still need to imagine some meta-mechanism generating that mind is just our own weakness; perhaps that mechanism exists only in the form of primordial dust, or is even a non-physical working out of logical possibilities? These problems must be tackled by the individual in his own terms. What matters is that we have taken the usual materialist world view, and we have examined it closely and found loopholes which will allow magic to take place: it was basically the same technique which allowed divination to 'work' once we admitted that 'there was a thing called the unconscious mind'.

It is as though the materialist was someone who lived on the London underground railway system and only admitted that the underground map was reality. We have examined it, observed the blank spaces and speculated about the streets that might lie in those blank spaces. We have gained a lot of freedom, new worlds to explore. But as long as we merely extend or add to that underground map we will be in error. Because the map is in a sense 'false'. Quite apart from the limitations of projecting three dimensions onto two, the London underground map is in fact a topological distortion: it has been bent to make it easy to read, wiggly lines have been made straight and distances falsified. We may find out much more than the materialist, but we can get very confused trying to fit our discoveries onto the old map.

Once more we are led back to the Abyss, we cannot forever dabble in sorcery. The only real freedom is via High Magic.

Don Juan describes this in Castaneda's 'Tales of Power'. He talks of our subjective reality and uses the word 'tonal' to describe it. He says the tonal is like a table in a restaurant, because it is, on inspection, similar to the other tables (ie. other people's reality). We assume it is 'true' and think there is nothing else (cf. 'General Psychic Relativity'). The sorcery I have described is equivalent to the discovery that one has the freedom to re-lay the table to some extent as one wishes.

But Don Juan draws attention to the greater reality beyond those tables, calling it the 'nagual'. Sooner or later we must learn to jump off the table and see the reality beyond. This corresponds to our idea of recognising our reality as just another map, and jumping off it.

We are paying a lot of attention to the sorcery stage; is this right? The mystic would say no, one cannot go on dabbling without risking being seduced by illusion; one must jump while one can. But as magicians it seems natural to explore the table as best one can before jumping off. Each time we come back to the Abyss, we do so with more experience and understanding. It may be illusion, but it's fun and it fills books.with words. We hope it prepares us better for the final jump, even if only by convincing us of its necessity.

21

THE INEVITABLE CHAPTER ON LOVE AND SEX

Learn then, o my Son, that all Phenomena are the Effect of
Conflict, even as the Universe itself is a Nothing expressed as the
Difference of two Equalities, or, an thou wilt, as the Divorce of
Nuit and Hadit. So therefore every Marriage dissolveth a more
material, and createth a less material Complex; and this is our
Way of Love, rising ever from Ecstacy to Ecstasy. So then all
high Violence, that is to say, all Consciousness, is the spiritual
Orgasm of a Passion between two lower and grosser Opposites.
Thus Light and Heat result from the Marriage of Hydrogen and
Oxygen, Love from that of Man and Woman, Dhyana or Ecstacy
from that of the Ego and the non-Ego.

                              CROWLEY - LIBER ALEPH

H what fun to smash the world up, kill tyrants, tear up
maps, rearrange tables! That's what anarchy is all about,
or so the papers tell us. So we don't really want to waste
much time talking about rebuilding structures.

Let us just look at these alternatives: if you are thinking of
adopting a belief you can choose a famous one, or a cranky one, or
you can make your own. A big famous belief from a reliable source
can be convincing and effective, but is likely to inspire awe and take
you over. A cranky belief is better in this respect: it is more of a
'throwaway' belief to suit one's mood. Cranky beliefs are found in
little books published by unheard of publishers, and are only sold
in rather odd bookshops - (hello? my ears are burning). Most
effective of all, and yet most seductive, is to invent your own
system of beliefs. There are of course no rules for this, so we

LOVE AND SEX

decided to give an example in action. Of course, as always in this book, it is not the end point that matters, but rather the process that it illustrates and the possibility it reveals.

We will invent a theory of ...... wait for it ... LOVE.

We start from the materialist notion used before: that all phenomena of the real world can be described, and so can be represented as a pattern, or, if you like, a circuit diagram, or logic network, or whatever.

Imagine tuning a pipe against another pipe: when they are perfectly in tune they sound together as one. If there are two pianos in a room and I play a note on one, the corresponding string on the other piano will vibrate in sympathy. This resonance we call 'love', and we state that:-

WHEN TWO PATTERNS ARE IDENTICAL THEY WILL RESONATE. THIS RESONANCE IS CALLED 'LOVE'.

Do you know how pipes are tuned? Two pipes sounded separately can be brought roughly in tune by ear. Then they are sounded together. If they are out of tune they clash and we hear a third sound: a throbbing beat. The closer they come to being in tune, the faster and more unpleasant is this beat; until they are exactly in tune, and it vanishes. This throbbing beat we call 'hate', and we state that:-

WHEN TWO PATTERNS ARE NEARLY BUT NOT EXACTLY IDENTICAL THEY WILL CLASH. THIS DISSONANCE IS CALLED 'HATE'.

As with the pipes which sound as one pipe, the resonance of love is felt as a yearning for one-ness. Hate is most painful when closest to the state of love. For example consider colours: two colours, such as two shades of red, nearly but not quite the same, will jar when placed together. Only when identical will the boundary vanish and they become one. Hate has given way to love.

But what about the attraction of opposites?

A world that can be described in words can be described in binary terms. So any pattern will have a precise anti-pattern, found by replacing all the negative values by positive, and vice versa.

Two such patterns superimposed will exactly cancel out,

96

mutually annihilate each other. This process we call sex, and
state that:-
       'WHEN TWO PATTERNS ARE EXACT COMPLEMENTS OF
EACH OTHER, THEY WILL COMBINE TO ANNIHILATE EACH
OTHER. THIS ACT WE CALL THE ACT OF 'SEX'.
       This complementation is felt as a yearning for mutual
annihilation.
       In the colour example we saw how two identical reds were
in love, but two different reds were in hate. If we now take two
opposite colours eg. red and green, we get an exciting, sexy
combination. But if we take two not quite opposite colours like
green and orange we again have a nasty effect. Just as two near
but not exactly matched patterns are in hate rather than love, so
are two nearly but not exactly complementary patterns in a state
of what we call 'fear', rather than 'sex'. So we state that:-
       TWO PATTERNS NEARLY, BUT NOT EXACTLY,
COMPLEMENTARY WILL CLASH. THIS DISSONANCE IS
CALLED 'FEAR'.
       Remember that unity is the symbol of love: the One God
is a god of love. But hatred guards the gates of love: nobody can
hate like the worshippers of a god of love.
       Remember that duality is the symbol of sex: the two horned
god is the god of sex. Fear, in the form of a serpent, guards the
gates of sex because sex is the urge to mutual annihilation, or
death. This is why the secret colour of sex is black.
       In a sense, of course, both love and sex mean annihilation:
the former a melting loss of individual identity, the latter an
explosive act. But we associate the latter more with our idea of
'death', the former is more like our idea of mystical transcendence.
The unique quality of the sexual annihilation is that it is not 'silent',
it gives birth to some third principle - a burst of energy or a 'child'.

       So far we have defined love, sex, hatred and fear as absolute
states that either exist or do not. Can there be degrees of strength?
       Any human being, if it really is a pattern, must be a pattern
of unimaginable complexity. All we can ever do is to break it down
into observable sub-patterns - its hairstyle, its voice, its gestures,

LOVE AND SEX

its education, its religion, its race, etc. - and even subdivide
again and again, so that at any moment we are only working in
a small area, containing just as much as we can comprehend.

Now all these infinities of sub-patterns are themselves
patterns, capable of being in love, sex, hate, or fear. Although
those states are absolute, their effect is additive.

Any two humans must have something in common, the very
fact of both being human constitutes 'an atom of love'. But, in
certain pairs, so many different sub-patterns resonate between
the two, that the overall impression of love is dominant at
certain times. It is this cumulative effect which makes the love
seem stronger: they are 'in love'.

In practice we usually mix love and sex; the real feeling
we call 'being in love' is an exciting combination of love and sex.
Some things are in common, and one has yearnings for oneness;
some things are contrary, and one has yearnings for nothingness;
the feelings merge and overlap in a tapestry of delight. In such
complex patterns as humans it would be statistically impossible
for there to be no elements of fear and hate between the two; but,
if love and sex are so dominant, the former are overwhelmed, or
merely spice the mixture.

That then is the bare bones of the theory, which must now
be fleshed with experience.

Lea had a theory about 'bobbies' and 'cops'. He loved the
British Bobby on his bicycle: Ernest the Policeman in the Toytown
children's broadcast used to blow his tiny mind. But he hated cops.
To his mind, the British police began to dig their grave when they
went from black Wolseley cars to white 'Z' cars in imitation of the
American Cop. Behind a wall of flashing lights and technology,
their image changed from quaintly human bobby, to sinister cop.
Cops snarl, drive fast, flash lights and kick open doors. Bobbies
say"'Ere, 'ere, 'ere,''and take your name in a notebook; they also
tell you the time. If you see a bobby being attacked you defend him
as a friend. If you see a cop attacked you admire the attacker's
courage.

When I took Lea to Middle Earth, and the police raided it,

and he saw a grim faced policewoman kick open a door, something clicked in his mind. I was meant to be the freaky teenage rebel, but I found myself holding back my peppery old uncle who was laughing out loud, and wanting to hug that coppess.

Lea hated cops because they were so close to something in the depths of his being, but they just missed it. What could have been Big Love came out as Big Stink.

Hate can wear one down, shake one to bits. It can also be a spur to glory etc. (yawn, yawn), but let's assume it hurts for now. Then the right understanding of the situation (a euphemism for believing what I tell you) can change that hate to liberating love.

What you do when burning in hate is scan the horizon with your binoculars, till you see a sign with 'Awe' written on it (it is usually in the direction of the sunrise), and you follow that sign.

Fear too can be a problem - no kidding. Recently I was faced with the horror of having to do some public speaking. Each morning I awoke with the cold fist of terror clutching at my vitals. Public speaking is so very much not me, it is <u>almost</u> my antithesis - see?

In morning meditation I struggled in vain to banish the chill wind that turned all to icy hell. Then I started to reason that if fear was the guardian of sex, was that perhaps the route to liberation? Gradually I clarified the nature of the antithesis, and removed its slight imperfection with analysis and adaptation. It began to look pretty sexy: me the phallic pillar standing and spouting into the warm receptive ears of the hungry mob - a sort of big scale exhibitionism! Yahoo! now a new problem - will I spray my pants when I do it? Oh well, at least it is different.

What you do when freezing in fear is to scan the horizon for a sign with 'Fascination' written on it (usually in the direction of the sunset) - follow that sign.

22

I'LL SING YOU TWO-O

I close my eyes and see a flock of birds. The vision lasts a
second or perhaps less; I don't know how many birds I saw. Were
they a definite or an indefinite number? This problem involves
the question of the existence of God. If God exists, the number is
definite, because how many birds I saw is known to God. If God
does not exist, the number is indefinite, because nobody was able
to take count. In this case, I saw fewer than ten birds (let's say)
and more than one; but I did not see nine, eight, seven, six, five,
four, three, or two birds. I saw a number between ten and one,
but not nine, eight, seven, six, five, etc. That number, as a whole
number, is inconceivable; ergo, God exists.
                    J. L. BORGES - DREAMTIGERS

When we try to examine the mirror in itself we eventually detect
nothing but the things reflected by it. When we wish to grasp the
things reflected, we touch nothing but the mirror. This is the
general history of knowledge.
                    NIETZSCHE - THE DAWN OF DAY

THE end is nigh.
Well actually we meant the end of this book — that is why our
weary pens are growing whimsical with anticipated relief.
That is why our conscience towards our readers and supporters
insists that we pause to give them something for their money. In
other words, it is time we told them what is wrong with the world
and what to do about it.

One of the most obvious things wrong with the world is too
many people with too many ideas on the subject. So we must make

an effort not to be original or creative, and merely add to the clamour. Instead we put our ears to the ground and listen to what others say.

In Septem Sermones Ad Mortuos, sermon IV we find:

"For me, to whom knowledge hath been given of the multiplicity and diversity of the gods, it is well. But woe unto you, who replace these incompatible many by a single god. For in so doing ye beget a torment which is bred from not understanding, and ye mutilate the creature whose nature and sign is distinctiveness ...."

What is meant by 'distinctiveness'? The first sermon describes a process of creation out of a nothingness called the Pleroma. Creation out of nothingness is inconceivable. The nearest we can approach to it is to conceive creation of pairs of opposites: out of nothingness there appears a pair of equal and opposite qualities, such as a positive and a negative charge. Then he says:

"The pairs of opposites are qualities of the pleroma which are not, because each balanceth each. As we are the pleroma itself, we also have all these qualities in us. Because the very ground of our nature is distinctiveness, therefore we have these qualities in the name and sign of distinctiveness, which meaneth –

"1. These qualities are distinct and separate in us one from the other; therefore they are not balanced and void, but are effective. Thus are we the victims of the pairs of opposites. The pleroma is rent in us.

" 2. The qualities belong to the pleroma and only in the name and sign of distinctiveness can and must we possess and live them. We must distinguish ourselves from qualities. In the pleroma they are balanced and void; in us not. Being distinguished from them delivereth us.

"When we strive after the good and beautiful we thereby forget our own nature, which is distinctiveness, and we are delivered over to the qualities of the pleroma, which are pairs of opposites. We labour to attain to the good and beautiful, yet at the same time we also lay hold of the evil and the ugly, since in the pleroma they are one with the good and the beautiful. When, however, we remain

true to our own nature, which is distinctiveness, we distinguish
ourselves from the good and the beautiful, and, therefore, at the
same time, from the evil and the ugly. And thus we fall not into
the pleroma, namely, into nothingness and dissolution."

The main significance of this will be discussed later, but
I would just like to draw attention to our earlier discussion of
'stripping off one's labels'. I hope it is clear that we recognise
that labels, or qualities, are <u>fun</u>, but that the danger is to <u>identify</u>
with those labels (rather than to 'distinguish oneself from them').
In the terms of the last chapter: if you are <u>one</u> with your sub-
patterns you will be <u>dominated</u> by the hates and fears of
misalignment, which would otherwise just be the spice of existence.
The example that was given earlier was the example of Economics:
of how an all-out dedication to the god Efficiency has almost
ground us to a halt.

Pressing our ears back to the ground we hear a rising cry
that for the past two thousand years at least, the West has been
dominated by an all-male god. The feminine has been devalued,
repressed or ignored; and an imbalance has resulted which must
be corrected.

One of the most eloquent expressions of this view ('Only
Two Can Play', by James Keys) is not to hand; but I recall that it
saw fault in the total acceptance of an all male god by the Christians
amongst others. This fault can be traced to Jewish origins, but
this could be unfair, because the earliest mentioned god in the bible
is, I believe, one which in the Jewish is made up of male and female
significators and so is really hermaphrodite, but has been translated
into male terms by the Christian interpreters.

Keys, and others, associates this unbalanced reverence
towards the masculine with a corresponding imbalance towards
'masculine' qualities such as analytic logic (at the expense of
feeling), aggression (at the expense of sympathy), knowledge (at
the expense of understanding) and so on.

From a different starting point, that of brain physiology,
we find a similar conclusion in Ornstein's book on the subject.
He sees a distinction in the working of the two halves of the human

102

brain, a similar distinction into 'masculine' and 'feminine' thought
processes; and he feels that western culture, and so the present
world order, is too heavily committed to the 'masculine' side at
the expense of the feminine.

Crowley's rejection of the Christian god is too well known
to need to be quoted, but it is interesting that he presents the idea
in a simpler form elsewhere; a form whose simplicity amounts to
an extension and generalisation of the analysis. In expanding his
theory of nihilism he sees it as an essential evolution of man's
thought: pantheism reached its highest form in Dualism, where
gods existed in complementary pairs. Monism appeared to be
a 'higher' truth as it continued the process of reduction (from
many, to two, to one) but in fact was a failure. In its best form –
the advaita philosophy of India – it recognised that the ultimate was
a non-existent nothingness, but still made the mistake of calling
it 'One'.

Crowley's nihilism, like that of the VII Sermones, begins
with an utterly unutterable nothingness from which pairs of
opposites can spring into manifestation – he symbolises it with the
equation $0=2$ – and we find the number 'one' is bypassed in the
process.

But has not the VII Sermones talked about the pleroma as
one thing, giving it a name? No, it is very good on this point.
The book should be read for it makes it quite clear that the pleroma
is utterly nothing, nothing can be said about it, all that is said about
it only tells us something about ourselves. Why was the first
Sermon written then? "Since, however, thought estrangeth from
being, that knowledge must I teach you wherewith ye may be able
to hold your thought in leash." A very Thelemic justification!

What does $0=2$ give us? out of nothingness a duality.
Duality is, in occult tradition, the mother of consciousness and
all that that entails. Do we have to accept this?

The first interesting point is that the above mentioned James
Keys is also author (as G. Spencer Brown – his real name) of a
brilliant book called the 'Laws of Form'. This is a difficult book on
mathematical logic, but it is also an exercise in extreme economy
of concept. In it the author begins with a single operation: namely

a splitting, or division into two, and argues that in that single
operation a universe is created. We find that familiar ingredients
of consciousness, such as memory and number, follow automatically from that act. Just as the I Ching argues all creation from
the initial separation into yin and yang, and the Kabbalah deduces it
from the creation of the three supernals, so does The Laws of Form
begin this task in the formal logical manner, creating the logic as
it proceeds.

So, for those who like the backing of authority, I present the
above three versions: I Ching, Kabbalah and Laws of Form. But,
for those who prefer reflection, I suggest the following meditation
on the birth of consciousness. The birth of consciousness can be
considered at the moment of creation itself, or as an event upon
our earth in an evolutionary timescale, or as an event in infancy
in a human timescale. According to the occult maxim of 'As above,
the like below', we would expect these three events to be the same
in essence. So let us imagine a baby becoming conscious.

To be preconscious is to be at one with the world, to share
all its moods: the world is hot, it is cold, it is nice, it is hungry,
it is hurting. Certain feelings have certain consequences: the
'want-tit-suck' mood is followed by 'tit-suck'; the two moods are
thus really not two, but just one continuum with all moods.

But then one day, one accursed day, oh day of wrath,
'titsuck' does not follow 'want tit suck' as mother is busy (there
always has to be a woman at the bottom of it all (ha ha)). In the
old order this is outrageous, it is inconceivable, the world has
been stopped. There is tit wanting to be sucked (of course),
movement towards it is rebuffed.

The only solution to this impossibility is a whole new order
of existence; a universe is created. Suddenly babe is not part of tit,
and tit is not part of babe. They are separate, and 'want tit suck'
is on this side of the abyss. Shit.

This act of creation must spring from bitterness and
frustration, and this shows in the consequences. This new 'out
there' world is separate from 'me here', and has its own stubborn
will that so often opposes poor babe. But consciousness has been
born and (don't worry folks) babe will get his own back on existence

104

by becoming a doctor of philosophy - music please.

Note that, in the terms of the last chapter, this birth of consciousness is analogous to the 'fall'. The state before was a state of total identity and so of undivided 'love'. The splitting of the world and creation of duality brings the first possibility of sex. The babe has eaten of the tree of knowledge and now sees itself as naked - alone against the world. He is no longer able to dwell in the Garden of Eden.

For those who do not trust such imaginary explanations I suggest that they try telling children that space before the big bang was one great big vacuum. The children will want to know what lies 'beyond' space, where it 'ends'. They don't like to be told that it does not end. If a mind tries to contemplate oneness it always rushes to find the edges, or limits; but give it a boundary, however simple and it can bounce to and fro happily, playing cosmic tennis. Tell yourself that the universe is a battle between Good and Evil, or a tissue of positive and negative charges, and the mind is as happy as a child in a sandpit. Consciousness just cannot survive on unity; duality is the minimum 'atom' of consciousness.

So by three approaches we have supported the idea of creation of consciousness, and therefore of manifest reality, being an act of drawing duality out of nowhere. So the number 'two' existed before the number 'one'.

What has this to do with male and female deities?

Tradition ascribes the number one to the male and the number two to the female. The figure one stands up like the phallus while two is curved and soft. The one penis and the two breasts. A lone god is always masculine. If a goddess is in that position, she is always a more or less disguised duality: she is given a pair of horns or a dual nature that flows between mother and seductress, or creator and destroyer (because of the mental link between sex and death illustrated in the last chapter).

The birth of consciousness was seen as a birth from frustration and bitterness - parturition and pain are close - the sea as female deity is called 'mare' which is related to the name 'Mary', the word 'marah' for bitterness and the sound 'mama'.

The sea is bringer of life and death in its different moods.

As James Keys reminds us, it is an obvious fib to have a male deity giving birth to a world, or Adam created first and Eve being made out of his rib - how far fetched! Only the woman can come first and give birth to the male, for only a woman has a womb. The story of the rib is a very poor repair job on a duff mythology.

In our recent attempts to convince ourselves that the male is the original sex we have reversed the usual order of nature, and made woman be the decorative sex. This has to be done via clothing and adornment, because the smooth female form is less able to be transformed than the male form with its prominent and developable musculature. What is more, the different nature of physical maturation of the two sexes means that if woman bears the burden of being the adorner, then an unnatural and rather cruel emphasis has to be placed upon youthfulness. Man as the attracter could at least relax and take his time (many men need wrinkles and a few grey hairs to look their best), whereas woman feels panicked into making it before her mid twenties, when the essentially female elements of beauty begin to grow less prominent.

In its simplest terms, therefore, we can ascribe many of the present ills of the world to our tendency to elevate unity above duality, even to the point of making a devil of duality.

In the terms of the last chapter, Love - the essence of unity - has been elevated at the expense of sex - the essence of duality.

"Woe unto you who replace the multiplicity of gods by one god." We have failed to distinguish ourselves in our striving after a god of love and we have fallen into its opposite, sex and fear. We have bred like flies and overpopulated the world, whereas the voluptuous natives of the south sea islands managed a stable population - not by cannibalism, it should be pointed out.

Brahma, Krishna, Allah, Jehovah, Christ and all the masculine absolutes will rise in protest at these theories. Their followers will show how in each case behind the duality there stood a greater unity. There is the pleroma itself. Crowley's 0=2 is

symbolised by the <u>one</u> equation. Spencer Brown's splitting into two
is <u>one</u> act of creation. Before the baby created the universe he was
at <u>one</u> with it in potential. So we cannot but admit the predominance
and pre-existence of unity.

But surely there is an illusion here? Before there was two
there was no consciousness to realise the one: it was not real. It
needed the consciousness to look backwards and to make it real, or
to create it. It is only the mind which says there <u>must have been</u>
a one before, which <u>names</u> the one act of creation. One was the
last number to be created: it needed the whole of consciousness to
give it birth. The Laws of Form did not write itself, it needed
the very sophisticated brain of G. Spencer Brown to work back to
such simplicity. It is only the fully developed consciousness
which later sees that first division as a division into two <u>units</u>.

It is as though we had returned to gaze at the still surface
of the primordial ocean and seen our reflection therein. "Look!
See! There lies one god beyond that surface!" But that god is
created in our own image, not vice versa. Statements made about
the pleroma are statements about ourselves, as it says in the VII
Sermones Ad Mortuos.

If we accept such diagnoses of the world's ills what is the
solution? Should, as some might suggest, the pendulum swing
back to the worship of the mother goddess and with it the associated
reinstatement of duality and sexuality?

Yes, it would be lovely. It does seem that societies like
Sweden who really make a hobby out of sex do manage to curb
excessive breeding; while the rigid sexual codes of India and
Victorian England beget multitudes.

As we have seen in chapter 20 it is our tendency to fall for
a single map of reality, or god, and to identify with it to the point
of enslavement, that lies behind our lack of freedom. It is the
rigidity of pure logic that does not admit the possibility of feeling
one's way onto other maps, which ties us to that one reality.

All these vices could be balanced and softened by a return
to the ways of the past. But even Lea, the rabid archaeoholic,
would admit that the spiral of evolution is perhaps better than the

return of the pendulum. If we do turn back, it should be a return on a new higher level, or else the errors of the past will simply repeat themselves.

If we accept the warning in VII Sermones, it is ultimately no better to strive after a goddess than a god, if you fail to distinguish yourself from either. There is no doubt that the male god, even if our own creation, is quite a guy and has done a lot for us. It would be a pity to give the poor sod the boot without so much as a 'thank you'.

So let us love him (that was all he ever asked for) and recognise him for what he is - our highest creation. As such he needs no worship, simply recognition and respect. Let us not be ruled by the ultimate reality, let us recognise this as another map of our own creation. The final sermon of VII Sermones tells us that the only god that really needs our worship is the inner star of our own individual being, our distinctiveness, a concept that immediately suggests the thelemic 'True Will'.

We can now stand apart from our gods and goddesses as distinct beings. Is this not a new birth? Like a growing child mankind first identifies with mother, then with father. In the name of science, we are apparently rebelling against father, but, as with teenage rebellion, it is merely a submission to the authority of fashion. The time has come to leave the home and stand on our own; it is a birth in that it is a separation from the womb of the family.

No longer identifying with the parents we stand separate, putting an emphasis on man as a separate being. Crowley called the coming age the Age of Horus, Horus being the crowned and conquering child. In his trinity, Nuit would correspond to the feminine deities, Hadit to the male, and now Horus stands apart as the child.

How can we equate the young adult leaving home with the child? From my own observation the stage after teenage rebellion is a partial return to childlike behaviour. No longer are we so self conscious, no longer is there such pressure to be 'cool' and adult. This is the age of the College Rag Day; when hairy rugger players dress up in drag and have perambulator races through town and other such embarrassing excesses. The Age of Horus could be a real hoot.

Rudolf Steiner saw Nietzsche as a prophet of the need for man to stand up for himself amongst the gods. Steiner himself broke away from the Theosophical Society to form his own Anthroposophical Society whose name reflects his own belief that the new spirit should begin with man and not god. He said that creation had proceeded from spirit into matter, completing that movement in the time of ancient Greece; from thence evolution must turn back toward the spirit. In that first phase it was right for man to see himself as a projection of God's will reaching down to matter, but now we should stand with our feet firmly in the material world and reach up using our own strength of will, not God's.

If this chronology is acceptable we should expect to find evidence of a free spirit doctrine being preached before the present age. Indeed we find examples in the earliest Christian gnostic writings. Carpocrates is quoted by Irenaeus in Adversus Haereses (180 A.D.) as having said that there is no 'good' or 'bad' except in human opinion; that one is here on earth for experience, and unless all acts, both good and evil, are practised in their fullness we will have to reincarnate in order to complete our experience. Freedom is to be beyond good and evil.

In Cohn's delightful 'The Pursuit of the Millenium' the history of such ideas in the Middle Ages is traced. I quote from his book two of many examples. The mystic Ruusbroec wrote:

"When I dwelt in my original being and in my eternal essence there was no God for me. What I was I wished to be, and what I wished to be I was. It is by my own free will that I have emerged and become what I am. If I wished I need not have become anything and would not now be a creature. For God can know, wish, do nothing without me. With God I have created myself and I have created all things ...... Without me nothing exists."

In the 17th Century the Ranter Clarkson wrote:

"till acted that so-called 'sin', thou art not delivered from the power of sin".

Jacob Boehme in 'Of the Supersensual Life' wrote:

"Son, when thou art quiet and silent, then thou art as God
was before nature and creature; thou art that which God then was;
thou art that whereof he made thy nature and creature."

Later he says: "If thou wilt be like all things, thou must
forsake all things ...... For as soon as ever thou takest something
into thy desire, and receivest it into thee for thine own, ... then
this very something is the same with thyself ...... and thou art
bound to protect it and to take care of it, even as of thy own being."

This is the same thesis as that described by Austin Spare
in the chapter 'Preface to Self Love' in his 'Book of Pleasure'.
Spare too called himself a 'supersensualist'.

But there is no need to assume a physical transmission
of these ideas down the ages - that need is an invention in the
yawn-armoury of materialism where it is wrongly believed that
information is a form of energy. After all the VII Sermones was
itself an automatic writing dictated by Basilides who was one of
those early Gnostics.

A basic element of Gurdjieff's teaching, and one shared by
his disciples, is the idea of 'waking up', of holding on to that vivid
clear consciousness which is not prey to negative emotion. This
is something like a vivid recognition of one's own being as opposed
to identification with qualities - a vice for which he used the term
'considering'.

Austin Spare gives under 'Definitions' in his 'Book of
Pleasure' the following:

"The words God, religions, faith, morals, woman etc.
(they being forms of belief) are used as expressing different 'means'
as controlling and expressing desire: an idea of unity by fear in
some form or another which must spell bondage - the imagined
limits: extended by science which adds a dearly paid inch to our
height: no more."

Here again we have religion, morality and science seen as
'imagined limits' giving a 'unity by fear'. On the next page he
writes:

"Some praise the idea of Faith. To believe that they are
Gods (or anything else) would make them such - proving by all they
do, to be full of its non-belief. Better is it to admit incapacity or

TWO - O

insignificance, than reinforce it by faith; since the superficial
'protects' but does not change the vital. Therefore reject the
former for the latter. Their formula is deception and they are
deceived, the negation of their purpose. Faith is denial, or the
metaphor of Idiocy, hence it always fails. To make their bondage
more secure, Governments force religion down the throats of
their slaves, and it always succeeds; those who escape it are but
few, therefore their honour is the greater. When faith perishes,
the 'Self' shall come into its own. Others less foolish, obscure
the memory that God is a conception of themselves, and as much
subject to law. Then, this ambition of faith, is it so very
desirable? Myself I have not yet seen a man who is not God
already."

This rejection of faith is very interesting, as it is yet
another warning about the limits of sorcery: in this early part of
the book Spare is very much arguing for High Magic. It is not
enough just to believe in the falsity of our reality, and to opt to
believe in other maps of reality, or magical theories, he says;
this is just delusion. We will remain slave to that original reality
until it is shattered, the Abyss has been crossed. Do you remember
the heady early days of psychoanalysis when we used to believe
that once you had 'discovered' that your fear of women was really
due to a childhood rejection by your mother, then that fear was
conquered? But how often do we find such cures working nowadays? Nietzsche had warned us about this when he wrote in the
'Dawn of Day':

"Because we see through a thing we think that, in future,
it will be unable to offer us any resistance whatever – and we are
surprised at finding we are able to see through it, and yet unable
to run through it. This foolish sensation and surprise are similar
to the sensation which a fly experiences before a window pane."

Again in SSOTBME we find a rejection of the absolute
reality or 'truth' of science and an advocacy of freedom of belief,
of using belief rather than being used by it. In this book we do
not just find this idea being recommended, but we also find the
suggestion that it is a change which will take place anyway by a
process of evolution of man's thought. It is suggested that just as

religion is losing its hold on man, leaving us free from morality and god, so too will science lose its hold, leaving us free from the tyranny of truth - the new 'god'.

When was it that morality caught its terminal sickness? Was it not when it was codified, and pinned down? Morality that depends upon individual judgement is a vigorous living thing; but when morality becomes equated with a rigid code of law and dogma then it is no longer part of us, we are 'distinct' from it and can grow free. The church did mankind the favour of thus enslaving morality long, long ago.

But the same is true of truth: subjective truth, depending on individual judgement is a living lively thing. Who now has the hold on truth? The law courts and the scientists! But we are heading therefore towards a new definition of truth: truth is becoming 'that which does not produce a reaction on a lie detector'!

The new free spirits must overcome the fear of technology in the hands of government and recognise it for what it is: government in the hands of technology. Go on, by all means, appearing to resist the lie detector, but secretly welcome it as a liberating ally. For, if we live to define truth in these terms, then we will become free from it: truth will no longer be a tacky concept with overtones of decency. A truly free spirit would be able to say anything to a lie detector, for its function is 'really' to detect anxiety, ie. bondage. So a truly free spirit will create his own truth as he goes along. Johnstone used to tell us to pray for total machine government - only then will we have rulers with insufficient imagination to be jealous of our private lives.

Do you recall the terrible siege in the Swedish bank vault? (1973, I think.) For a week or so we were held in thrall by newspaper accounts of the two criminals who had taken hostages into a vault. We heard how the hostages were being raped and tortured by the crooks and how the valiant police with an army of psychologists were struggling to save them, or what was left of them.

Finally the crooks gave in and out came the hostages. But far from being shrivelled wrecks of humanity they came out happy and smiling and waving goodbye to the crooks. "We weren't

112

frightened", they said, "just afraid the police might do something silly." How very embarrassing for law and order, and for the press who had revelled in accounts of the screaming of tortured victims! But were they embarrassed? Not likely! The 'expert psychologist', when asked to explain, said, "Er, well, you see, er despite the fact that for nearly a century we have been explaining how terrible shocks can have a damaging effect on health and physical well being, it is of course true that after a really terrible shock sometimes you find people, er, apparently quite normal."

So the poor happy people were taken off to a psychiatric hospital to be re-educated into believing that they had had a horrible time, and that their friends the crooks were nasty.

At first that story annoyed me a lot. Why did the public not protest at this buffoonery? What if one came back from a lovely holiday at Butlin's, and there were state psychiatrists waiting to persuade you that you had in fact just escaped from Belsen? But now I realise that the great public indifference was a glorious display of contempt. If 'experts' can remodel even the past, then two fingers up to 'objective truth' !

So there we are - had I known how long it would take to solve the world's problems we would not have begun this chapter.

Unity is strength* - strength to oppress us.

Divide and rule - this is what our tyrants have taught us, so let us turn the tables and use it against them.

* Though created as benevolent institutions, trade unions have grown bloated without providing any observable increase in fun in our daily lives. The monster feeds on pain; why else alienate a potentially sympathetic public by withdrawing services in strikes when it would be so much simpler to refuse to charge for those services? The latter course, apart from reinforcing public sympathy, would be much more efficient as a lever on management. The fact that it is never resorted to by the unions is sufficient proof that they do not exist for the benefit of humans.

TWO - O

    Science, like religion and politics, is digging its own grave. Leave it alone and it will complete the job. Meanwhile have fun. Let the age of the crowned and conquering child be the hilarious meat-joy age suggested. It had better be sexy, or I'm not coming back.

23

A TALE OF THREE CURSES

BLOODY hell, Leasus Jesus, do we really have to sit
and wait? Let me tell you a tale of three curses.
New Scientist ran a feature on the Vietnam war, and the
atrocious weapons the USA were using in that war. Do you
remember the outcry in the British Press when the IRA used a
nail bomb? How we were told that this was the ultimate low in
degradation, sub-human, sub-animal, to use a shrapnel bomb
against one's fellow men? But do you realise that the US army
used shrapnel bombs with <u>plastic</u> pellets because they realised
that metal was too easily removed by surgery? It is no question
of defending terrorism, it is a question of getting one's priorities
right when seeking the enemies of mankind. The worst atrocity
possible for the IRA was not considered bad enough for use by the
US government - a government rated amongst the more humane
of its kind. Terrorism is merely the aping of one's rulers; as
the Taoist sage said, "Steal a purse and they will put you in jail,
steal a country and they will make you a Duke."

As I read of those horrors of war, wrath surged within me,
burning, consuming wrath. But I knew enough of alchemy not to
drink it. Then came the outcry that President Nixon had ordered
intensified bombing, in the face of world opinion against it. The
public rage reverberated with my rage. But I could see how those

who drank it merely drowned in its bitterness.

Fortunately I was out of work, on the dole, at home
stewing in my own bile. This emptiness is a condition of great
power - it is why cunning government chooses to keep people busy;
or at least, by propaganda, to make those out of work feel shame.
Shame is a veil to obscure naked power.

So in a torment of disintegration my reality weakened to the
point where, with encouragement, the thought that 'the universe
cannot possibly have been created such that one man is able to
deliver such pain and anger on a world without redress' became
as real as the old materialist thought that Nixon was far away out
of my reach. So I set a curse on him, allowing myself to be a
channel for the world's anger.

According to Johnstone's directions I had fulfilled the
first conditions: despair, strong desire contained, a cracking
point in reality. Now I had to separate myself from the desire –
attain non-attachment without weakening the original wrath by
letting it escape. As the alchemists say the theriac, or poison,
must be in a sealed vessel.

I used reason to seal the vessel. I reminded myself that
it was not Nixon, but New Scientist that made me angry. Having
myself practised not listening to the news, Nixon had no reality to
me except as a fashion word. I really had nothing against him.

The wrath took shape and I answered its questions but never
looked, so I could not become fascinated again. Should it kill
Nixon?

Now Johnstone had argued not. Assassination, he said,
was every ruler's dream, as it removed at a stroke the realisation
of his own incompetence and replaced it by the hope of posthumous
canonisation. On the contrary, the perfect end for a politician is
to find himself under the scrutiny of the very psychiatric police
force that he helped to found. Death is too glorious for politicians.

Sure enough there came to be times when Nixon flaunted
himself before the angry public against the advice of his bodyguards;
no doubt yearning for Manson's saints to act for him.

My only task was to direct without attachment. I pictured
the poison as a spinning top - stable because it was fast moving -
and would scan the news with half an eye. If any news was seen

which supported the cause, I just said a mental 'YES', like a whip cracking the top, and stopped reading.

But was it then I who caused his downfall? Beware the sticky tentacles of attachment, Angerford! Care not, no doubt others tried too. There is no distinction in moving with the tide of the times. The <u>object</u> of the exercise was not to hurt Nixon - who had no reality in my world - but to enlarge the crack in that tyrannical reality which told me that we were helpless pawns in the power of politicians. That worked - only in those terms do I claim success for my working.

Around the same time Concorde flew over Gloucestershire without sufficient silencing. It left a huge wake of noise, and induced anger. I found myself seething as the head-ringing thunder passed. In their calculations of the damage done by noise, did the economists and advisers make any allowance for the anger generated in the sufferer's mind?

In similar spirit to the other curse, but more spontaneous, I hurled the anger at the sky in a gesture-directed scream. As it left me I wanted to see the 'plane explode in flames but a voice said "Economics is the only weakness"; "so let it be" I replied in the flash.

Now that voice was a devil of my reality I now realise, but at least an honest devil that kept his word. But I had cast off my rage in one huge effort and was exhausted and free.

The same process maintained the curse.

The third torment was despicable treatment at the hands of the GCHQ in Cheltenham, as a result of which all my ideas as to the possible higher standards of British government were drowned. Here was another time of despair, a power potential in the sense of Austin Spare. But here was more difficulty.

Nixon was easy because he was not real - I knew nothing about him and didn't care. Concorde was more difficult because occasionally I saw it, it had a bigger claim to reality. But as I lived in Cheltenham overlooking the GCHQ establishment, and many neighbours worked there, it was hard to isolate it from my reality. I could not do it. Therefore it was subject to the laws of reality.

This meant that its destruction needed a magical link in the terms of that reality.

So I considered bombs on balloons, nerve gas, and bacteria. I investigated the geology of the area for an idea of the underground structure of the establishment; and considered geological warfare such as the diverting of underground springs, harnessing the Malvern slip where earthquakes have been recorded, and so on. I considered a continental trip to obtain rabies germs which could be administered to officials with an airgun. I considered going straight and retraining in catering, so I could get a job in their canteen and gently bend their minds. And so on and so forth, all the usual angry stuff that everyone dreams of.

But every dream rang false - it somehow was not me. On my horoscope nearly all the planets were setting: that was how it was - I was simply not an effective agent, not a creator of circum-stances. I could never do any of those things. The only planet not setting was Mercury. That told me that my only avenue for effective action on the world would be in writing or communicating. The only war I could ever wage successfully was ideological war. So was it possible to publicise a philosophy of life that would under-mine the very roots of secret government establishments? What do you think, dear reader?

Still slave to my reality, I could only work within it. We do not choose to make curses, circumstances make them inevitable. Comfort comes from moving with the times. Now I do not care. Good.

History supports the possibility. When you studied the surviving early christian gnostic fragments, Lea, did you not find a strong flavour of the Free Spirit at times? Is there not evidence, even in the Bible, of Christ preaching a free spirit doctrine in the face of the law? Has it not been argued that Christ was an advocate of the free spirit and that the institutionalised Christianity was nothing of his making? A travesty of his will? Few signs of free spirit teaching survive, not because they were few to begin with, but because they were purged. And Steiner was right: the ascent of

A TALE OF THREE CURSES

man was intended to begin at that time.

Then what destroyed the cosmic plan?

Once there was an angry young man who was obsessed with Jewish law. He saw it challenged by a sect, the followers of Christ, who preached freedom and love. The measure of his hatred was that he persecuted this sect relentlessly: he was in on the stoning of Stephen. Then on the road to Damascus he saw a blinding vision that asked "Saul, Saul, why persecutest thou me?" and told him that it was "hard for him to kick against the pricks", which has been interpreted as 'don't fight it, baby, _feel_ it'.

Then for three days he was blind and did not eat or drink. Then he was revived and he joined the Christians, and became St. Paul the founder of the established Christian church.

The vision he had seen said it was Christ. But visions must be regarded with extreme caution. In his 'Pursuit of the Millennium', Cohn quotes a vision of the Catholic mystic Suzo in 1330, a vision of an incorporeal being who sounds like the very angel of the free spirit. He speaks to it:

"Whence have you come?"

"I come from nowhere."

"Tell me, what are you?"

"I am not."

"What do you wish?"

"I do not wish."

"This is a miracle! Tell me, what is your name?"

"I am called Nameless Wildness."

"Where does your insight lead to?"

"Into untrammelled freedom."

"Tell me, what do you call untrammelled freedom?"

"When a man lives according to all his caprices without distinguishing between God and himself, and without looking before or after ....."

Now that vision was a scripture to me. It took a female mind to see through it. "Would you trust a vision that said that?" she asked. "If it was really like that, why did it need to reveal itself?"

Then I saw the concealed poison in the last sentence - we

are exhorted not to distinguish ourselves from God - the destruction of the true free spirit. Not to distinguish is to be for ever subservient, only by standing apart can we see ourselves as equals.

With infinite subtlety the fountain of truth is forever being poisoned - witness those commentators on Thelema who forget the capital 'W' in 'Do what thou Wilt'.

So do we believe it was Christ who zapped Paul? Is it Christlike to blind a man for three days and to describe your followers as 'pricks'? No! The vision was the pay-off of a demonic pact of the kind I have described in chapter 14. St. Paul should be the patron saint of the new revolutionary, for he swallowed his pride, sacrificed his public image, and joined the hated sect. He out-did them all - he took it over and destroyed it from within. As the dominant leader he changed the nature of Christianity (witness the purge of the free thinking elements described in later books of the New Testament), he made it into just another system of law. Who has ever managed such a thorough revenge? What greater example of applied hatred has ever been seen on earth? Two thousand years of buggered up humanity! No wonder God wept. No wonder the last book of the bible is a little, er, odd.

So it can be done folks. I, Satan's advocate, can bugger up the next two thousand years. In the name of Lemuel Johnstone horrors will be enacted ......

Oh Angerford, you naughty boy! Smack your little bottom! Why do you tell such fibs?

To save other people from thinking them?

To save other people from believing them?

To cast the great liberator, Doubt, back into the fray?

At some point in the story truth departs. By keeping the departure secret the reader is cast back to his own free judgement. The spider's web remains empty, beautiful and clean.

Say the worst, or others will imagine it.

24

THUNDERSQUEAK -
OR THE POLITICS OF DESPAIR

Brutally shall I teach the gospel of soul suicide
AUSTIN SPARE - THE ANATHEMA OF ZOS

IT is no good, every time we play with sorcery we find ourselves coming back to the same Abyss: our freedom is an illusion. We are still in the hands of a tyrant. That tyrant is an illusion, but that knowledge itself gives no freedom - it merely makes the tyrant seem even more beyond our power. Knowledge is Daath, the sephira of the Abyss itself; so it is not knowledge which will help us over the chasm.

What good have we done you? Our book has given you a few glimpses of freedom, a few moments of hope, before the secret brain police swooped. You are thrown in a cell in solitary confinement; but you go on expecting the revolution. You are starved, you are beaten; but your spirit fights on in solidarity with your friends outside. Then you are told that the revolution is over, that the rebels are all in gaol. Still you recall the words of Thundersqueak: you recall that the war can never be won. Then they start prescribing drugs, needles in the brain, flashing lights, sensory deprivation. Laughing and screaming like a maniac you hold out. Then they tell you all the other rebels have cracked, why fight on? You have not slept for a fortnight and your last fingernail is waiting to be drawn. But the image of Thunder-squeak keeps telling you "they cannot win, they cannot win". Then suddenly you realise that the image of Thundersqueak was all along telling you to give in, because it does not matter. So you do give in.

But, alas, your tormentors have also read Thundersqueak,
so they merely redouble their efforts. Your existence dissolves
in a shrieking maelstrom of alternate confession and resistance.

Then the authors of Thundersqueak are brought to you: seedy
little men in the uniform of the junta. With a certain simpering
gleefulness, they explain how Thundersqueak came to be written for
the junta. No ruler could forever survive rebellion, true. But what
if the ruler <u>created</u> the rebellion in the first place? The junta
decided that an essential element in its power would be to create
a revolutionary theory itself, to let the revolution crystallise onto
the seed implanted by themselves. Thundersqueak was a secret
government pamphlet. Thank you for your support.

Support. Support. Sup. Port. S. U. P. P. O. R. T.

Unmeasurable time of agony has taken its toll. You crack.
Something else is in your body. It loves Big Brother.

So that was it. May we tease you a little?

Do you remember how we once told you that the tyranny
could never really win, because those torturers were looking for
something and how could they know what they were looking for unless
it existed within their own minds? We suggested that when they
twist you till you crack, what have they done but banish that demon
to a region beyond their grasp - at least in you it was <u>contained.</u>

Why did those ideas offer you comfort as you screamed?
Because they were credible? Credible in terms of what? In
terms of the way you believed the world to be? You mean that had
we instead written 'tyranny cannot win, because God, who made the
world, is good' then you would not have been supported by our
writings? Poor fool! You only accepted us where we matched
your reality: where your tyrant allowed you to believe us. You get
the government you deserve. Your government gets the rebels
that it creates. But we still care.

Let us proudly assume that you would not have read this far
if you had not enjoyed it. So let us continue what we were doing
and see if, now you know what is happening, you still enjoy it. Then
to hell with the revolution!

Do you believe in the ultimate horror of science in the hands of the torturers? But there are many scientists who have studied the subject, and maintain that modern methods are no more effective than those of the Spanish Inquisition. The belief in Science has replaced the belief in God, and the strength of the result depends only upon the strength of the belief. In those days it was omniscient God who probed your soul, now it is omniscient Science.

There! We replaced one belief - the superiority of modern techniques, by another - doubts about that superiority. On with the game!

Judge for yourself: is it not stupid to attempt some objective measurement of hellishness? Surely there is only one absolute point - the point where a human mind disintegrates - and if that point is reached by any torture technique it is the point of absolute hell; and no other standard of hell can be applied. In these terms torture was 'perfected' ages ago: all that happens is that new techniques are needed to keep pace with new freedoms.

Now we see the measure of the torturer's power over us: it is the power to disintegrate a mind.

But what of those minds that disintegrate of their own accord? The asylums are full of them. Can we really say that any hell is worse than that of the raging lunatic? Somehow the image of the mighty torturer fades when we see him as merely the tool for a change in us: a change which might easily have happened of its own accord.

Even more bizarre is the realisation that many spiritual disciplines set out to produce that very disintegration, and that those disciplines are willingly embraced by their followers. But that realisation must be worked for. We can see that it was a bit tough for the tortured martyr when he realised that the very church he loved had been infected by the power of Satan, that his very support had been knocked away; but can we understand that this revelation was just as ghastly as might be the revelation under torture that fluoridation of water had in fact been a secret and successful government project to bring revolution into the open by altering the chemistry of our brains? The same feeling of utter helplessness in the face of adversity has the same power to crack you, wherever it comes from.

THUNDERSQUEAK

In chapter 22 we quoted Boehme. In the same tract he
describes the soul's path to liberation as a series of appalling
'descents into hell' where even God himself seems to desert the
soul. It brings to mind the torture technique of bringing the body
repeatedly to the point of death, then reviving it.

We also quoted some free spirit tracts from Cohn's 'Pursuit
of the Millennium'. Read that book and you will find a constantly
recurring theme of the 'descent into hell' that preceded the
liberation. I quote from Coppe's 'A Fiery Flying Roll' just brief
extracts to give the flavour of the whole:

"First all my strength, my forces were utterly routed, my
house I dwelt in fired; my father and mother forsook me, the wife
of my bosom loathed me, mine old name was rotted, perished; and
I was utterly plagued, consumed, damned, rammed and sunke into
nothing, into the bowels of the still Eternity (my mother's womb)
out of which I came naked and whereto I return naked." Already,
in present day terminology, we would give Coppe a stress number
of over 200. Sure enough he heard two terrible thunderclaps and
had a vision of God. But God had not done with him yet. When he
greeted God with joy, God said he must first "drink a bitter cup,
a bitter cup, a bitter cup; whereupon (being filled with exceeding
amazement) I was throwne into the belly of hell (and take what you
can of it in these expressions, though the matter is beyond
expression) I was among all the Devils in hell, even in their most
hideous hew." And yet, through hell, some little spark remained
even though, in his words, all life was taken from his body as if a
picture had been wiped out with one stroke. Then life returned
after four days and nights, and he was free.

How do we judge the result? How do we judge a freedom
beyond our understanding? Crowley would argue that Coppe's
error was to have allowed that one little spark to remain. In
Liber Cheth he writes:

"2. Thou shalt drain out thy blood that is thy life into the
golden cup of her fornication.

"3. Thou shalt mingle thy life with the universal life. Thou
shalt keep not back one drop.

"4. Then shall thy brain be dumb, and thy heart beat no more,

124

and all life shall go from thee; and thou shalt be cast out upon the
midden, and the birds of the air shall feast upon thy flesh, and thy
bones shall whiten in the sun.'"

What he goes on to describe is an utter tearing away of all
qualities. If reality cannot be abandoned in joy it will only be lost
with pain. Failing to live the truth of VII Sermones means that we
have identified with those elements of our reality, so that losing
them is the pain of losing one's being. Existence may well be pure
joy, but the chains we forge about ourselves deny existence and
deny joy.

Austin Spare's magical system was based upon the descent
into hell. Here is Johnstone's analogy of it: We picture ourselves
as a tree and our own individual condition as the tip of one tiny twig
on that tree. But we are dissatisfied, we wish to be a different tip
of a different twig. Can we achieve the total freedom to realise
that we are the whole tree anyway? All its branches, trunk and
roots are within us as the sedimentary strata of evolution -
traceable in our bodies and unconscious minds. If not, we must
travel inside ourselves back down the branch; until we reach a
point where we are joined to that other desired twig. Only then
can we move up the tree again to reach that state. Pure desire
toward that other state is sterile, we must regress, or descend,
as far as is needed. The more remote that desired twig, the
farther into hell, or down the tree, we must go.

But how can we get back? By exhausting ourselves in lust,
physical effort, despair or sorrow; anything as long as it takes
us back. Exhausted we reach a state of empty pre-consciousness
which Spare named 'the Death Posture'. Our present ego identity
is only the tiniest bud on the tip of the branch. Language and
human consciousness does not go far back down the twigs. So we
will be regressing beyond their domain.

This need to pass beyond the dualistic distinction of
conscious, logical, thought is illustrated in the technique Spare
called the 'neither-neither'. This is his version of the Zen Koan -
a nonsense phrase that is used for meditation; the reasoning
faculty is forced to work on the koan until it cracks. Spare reaches
towards this point in four steps. First you consider some quality,

let us say 'light'. Then you consider its polar opposite, in this case 'darkness'. Next you consider those two together, both light and darkness - the world as we know it. Then you consider the absence of either - neither light nor darkness. If this form of meditation is frequently practised, with various qualities, you can find that the attempt to conceive the inconceivable in the last stage, results in a sort of dizziness of consciousness that is brimming with potential.

But how then do we not lose our way? By encapsulating the desire in a form primitive enough to survive the descent: a mantra will only take us back to the origins of its language. Spare advocates his 'sigils', geometric forms constructed from the wording of the wish. He points out that before use we must 'forget' the sigil's purpose, or else it is tacky with associations, and will get stuck on the way down the branch.

So that is Spare's sorcery; yet his High Magic once again demands the the utter descent to the roots, the loss of all, so that we may gain the freedom of the whole tree.

How can he try to see value in annihilation and despair? Answer: because it is there.

While working in a nasty computer office I was often sick with 'flu and colds: one more agony in an already nasty job. It seemed like the last straw. But one day, as I sat at a computer terminal, it occurred to me that in my dead state I was actually better at the job because of having a cold. It made me more inert and less impatient. Times of 'flu were the only times I stopped worrying about 'what had to be done', and had a day in bed and wrote letters and read books. Perhaps the concept of minor illness was a mistake? Had we once again identified with one god or quality, ie. 'health', and so fallen into sickness as an 'evil'? Was not so-called 'sickness' just a state when we were better disposed to do other things? like lying in bed (and groaning)?

The symbol of Saturn is the symbol of death, frustration, humiliation and despair. These are associations that we have given to the symbol. But basically Saturn was the symbol for the limits of the solar system (being the original outermost planet) and so of our own limits. We identify with our limits and so they become limitations. When we get our M.A. we do not classify ourselves

any longer by our B.A. or our 'A' levels. We boast that we can
run a mile in four minutes, but we are too modest, for we are also
free to run a mile in any time <u>over</u> four minutes. I have an earning
potential of so many thousand, but I am also capable of earning any
figure well below that value.

In past ages Saturn was also associated with the breaking of
those limits: the Saturnalia was an orgy of gluttony and lust which
lies behind the present celebration of Christmas. Once again more
people associate Christmas with drunken licence than with prayer.
Some suggest that it was the Saturnian metal, lead, in the Roman
water supply that caused the breakdown of Roman civilisation; some
say Saturn has returned again in the form of leaded petrol fumes to
destroy our own civilisation. But we are no longer so ready to
associate such licence with Saturn, as he is no longer the true limit
but just our chosen limit. Beyond him lies Uranus, the magician,
Neptune, the mystic, and Pluto the bamalama bamalou (Crowley,
Steiner and Spare perhaps?).

The alchemical texts are consistent in describing the first
part of the great work as a 'blackening'. It cannot be avoided,
this path of Saturn, this descent into hell. We should not want to
avoid such an important part of existence; the desire to avoid it
is a symptom of our misunderstanding.

Johnstone described success as a rut, albeit a nice one.
Times of success are times of running along rails which were laid
down in times of depression. Look out for those low times and use
them.

The father of modern politics wrote in his autobiography
'Mein Kampf' of his moment of blackest despair when he heard of
Germany's surrender at the end of the first World War. "Everything went black before my eyes as I staggered back to my ward
and buried my aching head between the blankets and pillow ......
The following days were terrible to bear and the nights still
worse ...... During these nights my hatred increased ......"
Everything was shattered, and at that nadir he decided to go into
politics. That he did so with such effect, and that the payoff of
this particular pact required the sacrifice of his life and that the
result has been the birth of a new age in politics, has already been

said.

So when the brain police begin to turn the screw on you
remember this: that they are doing you a favour. All their techniques are ones that have been chosen by mystics of the past in
their search for transcendence. Isolation is the first requisite,
then fasting. Often one misses sleep, being told to pray continuously
and 'never relax vigil'. One's routine is upset, one is humiliated,
or humiliates oneself. One even scourges oneself, and blows one's
mind with sacred drugs. Sensory deprivation is enforced - sitting
for ages in utter stillness and cutting out all sense impressions. At
first you are supported by hope, the sense of novelty or purpose,
one's idea that God is with you. But as the process proceeds these
props crumble and one enters the 'Dark Night of the Soul' described
by all mystics.

This is what the brain police so lovingly prescribe for you.
Blessed are you to have it all served up on a plate!

Here is the recipe for escaping from the world that you
have created: the tyrant that you have voted into power.

Johnstone said that the only possible escape from the inertia of
General Psychic Relativity lay in the cuspal points of that very
inertia: the places where the density became infinite. In VII
Sermones the devil is described as the 'eternal, sucking void', a
good description of what science calls a 'Black Hole'.

A Black Hole is a point where the forces of gravity are so
high that matter collapses into itself. Not even light can escape
from such a place, hence the name 'Black Hole'.

Inertia, or mass, is so dense that all surrounding matter
is drawn in and collapses inwards. But where does it go? Scientists
speculate about 'white holes', or fountains of matter in other places
in space, but they do not in fact know.

Nor do the brain police really know what they will get as
they drive you into the black hole of your own psyche - confessions
perhaps, information perhaps, conversion perhaps? But what
trust can one put on information from a madman? Someone who has
undergone an initiation not undergone by themselves? What use is
a friendly lunatic? Hate has been fed, not utility.

How can we know what happens when we enter a black hole?

THUNDERSQUEAK

All measuring apparatus, all recording equipment, all brain cells
will collapse with the passage. All that might survive would be
non-material: perhaps a pattern, or awareness? So how can we
control or direct ourselves through such a journey? No control
mechanism can survive the trip; our only control could be the speed
and direction with which we enter the black hole. An arrow slot in
a castle is only inches wide, but by aiming through it the archer
has considerable scope for choosing his target.

The brain police need your mind to set that course. As
long as they can make you believe that you cannot win, they are
all powerful, and you will surrender and join them; then there is
hope that you will be on the right course for their desired objective.
But if you see the process as one of mystical transcendence, or a
test from God, what can they do? You can hold a geometric figure
like the cross before you as you descend into hell, and that symbol
is so elemental that it will survive way beyond the point where
language fails and reason fails. It too will eventually fail, but it
will have set your course across the Abyss.

We cannot control the passage, that is illusion. We have
to jump eventually. But even though our flight is an act of total
surrender, the last decision before we leap is the decision that
sets our course to the other side.

You were the lucky one, you had the call of freedom. The
brain police were a self defeating illusion that lay below the Abyss.
Or were they the High Priests of the Mysteries?

25

AFTER THE STORM

A king may choose his garment as he will: there is no certain test.
CROWLEY - THE BOOK OF THE LAW

HOW does it go, that saying to the effect that 'Before I heard
of Zen, a tree was a tree, a stone was a stone. When I
heard of Zen a tree was no longer a tree, and a stone no
longer a stone. Now I have attained Zen a tree is again a tree, a
stone once more a stone'? I wonder where Thundersqueak will
take us?

In the 'Pursuit of the Millennium' we read of the unconventional
behaviour of the free spirits. There were those who shunned
worldly trappings and went naked. Then there were those who dressed
as beggars to show how they despised their own status in life - as
with present fashion, courtiers wore clothes with fake tears and
patches in them. But then came free spirits who dressed as rich
nobles, saying they were so much above the things of the world
that they were free to indulge themselves without fear of being
tainted. Such behaviour was to the despair of a society that insisted
upon its members' status being reflected in their attire.

Do we not see a progression here? Should not the new free
spirit be utterly inconspicuous and all-pervasive? 'Lurk - as it is
written in the Book of the Law.' Let them be schoolteachers,
policemen, politicians, scientists or whatever; for they have nothing
to fear. Let them be recognisable only by their lightness and
laughter. Then let another generation arise which is free to
abandon even that sign of brotherhood.

When the secret police pull me out of my bed at three in the

morning, and punch me in the stomach, I will survey their granite
features and grim mouths with admiration. As they call me 'rebel
filth' and 'anarchist shit' I will be rejoicing within, but will never
reveal it. I will curse and struggle as in secret inner thought I say
"Oh my captors! you are so good! Just like the real thing! You
must be free spirits! No-one else could look that mean!" And, in
a funny sort of way, I'll be right.

"What some call hypocrisy, I call freedom of the spirit"
said Johnstone: it was probably his last wild, abandoned utterance
before he faded into mediocrity and death. But, when he said it,
there was a clap of thunder and the veil of the temple was rent
from top to bottom. A shudder ran through the corridors of so-
called 'power'. For a rebel that ceases to exist is a rebel that
cannot be crushed. It is a phantom that will haunt your weakest
moments, seeming to appear and disappear when it will. The
babe Harpocrates sits in silence on the lotus, finger to his lips.
"Mum's the word, don't worry about Dad."

Thank you, Lea. May the Great Mystery make Sunrise in
your Heart.

As destroyer, I cannot view our creation without misgivings.
Another book in a universe already stuffed with words. Have we
just given you a new set of ideas to tyrannise and torment you?
Will you be slaves to Right Wing Anarchy?

No ideas are ultimately good, not even our ones. Time then
to disillusion you, to show you the lunatic fringe of half-baked right
wing anarchist extremism.

How do we rule our inner kingdoms? At the absurd limits of
right wing anarchy is what Johnstone called 'the Royal Anarchist'.
Here is someone who claims that monarchy is not government, it is
art. In large societies, government is only possible by delegating
power, setting up a hierarchy. This is not true monarchy. A
monarch is a symbol who cares for the merely symbolic affairs of
state, leaving people in freedom. He is a social art form, the only
social art form.

For two thousand years we have been in the age of Pisces,
yet the one establishment that survived those two thousand years

was the one which recognised and incorporated the symbol of the
Virgin, ie. of Virgo, the opposing and balancing sign of the zodiac.
Similarly those anarchists who survive in the age of Aquarius will
be those who recognise and incorporate the symbol of the Magnificent
King, ie. the symbol of Leo, into their inner Kingdoms.

The concept of the Socialist State is a tyranny, because it
includes and therefore dominates us – we are part of it. But a
royal family or glorious Sun King is an object of love. We can
rejoice in the pageantry, be inspired without being diminished.
For the King is an art form of our own creation; a God that we
love because we know we made him.

How cheap it is to run a Royal Family compared with a Civil
Service! A few pence in the pound and you have the glories of
Buckingham Palace. How nice to know there are places we are
not allowed to visit, treasures we can only imagine, because we
want it that way. The present Royal Family may not match up
to Mr. and Miss Universe, but they are the best thing in the
constitution.

You have in your hands, dear reader, something very
bizarre, perhaps unique. A nihilist and anarchist tract that ends
with the words

'God save the Queen' !

26

EDITORIAL AFTERWORD

A philosophy is perhaps best judged not by its scriptures but by its followers. So perhaps you should know something about Liz Angerford and Ambrose Lea.

Lea degenerated into a bitter old man, quoting the Daily Express and complaining about the young. One day he took out his old services revolver, put it to his mouth, and supped the lead and cordite cocktail.

On that day Angerford got into a very, very fast car and went for a very, very fast drive down the wrong lane of a continental motorway. He chose the most expensive and official looking car on the road against which to pulp his physical existence.

What a laugh! The demon duo you've learnt to love to hate are nought but a pair of stinking stiffs! So much for Right Wing Anarchy!

Now my contribution as editor has been long and arduous, so I would like to allow myself a little old-fashioned indulgence in the last few pages. It is called 'respect for the dead'.

You see the Lea that pulled the trigger was not the Lea that wrote this book: the bird had flown, I know not where. The death of the body, which these two Leas shared, was a sort of re-birth for the Lea who wrote this book. For now I can remember the former Lea, without the embarrassing physical existence of a bitchy old man of the same name.

Angerford was an adrenalin tripper. He had often risked his life in accidents before, He had noticed an acceleration in his

133

EDITORIAL AFTERWORD

consciousness near the moment of death. He reckoned that if the last moments of existence were partitioned into an infinite series in 'objective' time, a series that converged upon the moment of death (for example: death minus one second, half second, quarter second and so on) and if it was found that the resulting partition of 'subjective' time formed a non-converging series (eg. one apparent second, half second, third second, fourth second, fifth second and so on) then one would experience immortality in an apparently finite framework, 'spiralling forever inward through a hole in time'.

On the car's paintwork he had scrawled 'We always will remember - Buddy Holly'. I like to believe that he made it.

So that is that. There is no-one very great chez The Mouse That Spins. I too must review this ragged work with shame. It is as inconsistent, lumpy, self contradicting, and inconclusive as life itself.

If you think then of this book as a book of failed ideas, then you will be free from being enslaved by it. We built bridges across to different realities, bridges to freedom. As with the parable of the finger pointing at the moon - it is the moon and not the finger you are supposed to observe - you should realise that it is not those other realities that were important, but rather the bridges that took you there. Having realised that you must blow up those bridges, for they are not important either. All that matters is that you should now realise the possibility of building your own bridges to freedom.

Had I made this book into a consistent and conclusive whole it could have been no greater than its creator.

The U.S. army gets round the rules about storing nerve gas by not storing nerve gas. Instead they store separate chemicals which combine to form nerve gas. We too can play that game. The unmixed ingredients in this book can combine in a suitable vessel to make a high explosive. You, reader, are greater than we ever were, so do it yourself. Let it happen.

One day there will be a great big BANG and you will be free. So will the world. But you already are. That is why this is

THE END

BIBLIOGRAPHY

Anon - 'S.S.O.T.B.M.E.' An Essay On Magic.
Boehme - On the Supersensual Life.
Borges - Dreamtigers.
Castaneda - Journey toIxtlan (and others).
Chuang Tzu - Works of.
Cohn - The Pursuit of the Millennium.
Crowley - The Book of Lies, Liber Aleph (and others).
Heard - The Wishing Well.
Jung - Septem Sermones ad Mortuos.
Keys - Only Two Can Play This Game.
Kuhn - The Structure of Scientific Revolutions.
Lao Tzu - Tao Teh Ching.
Nietzsche - Beyond Good and Evil, The Dawn of Day, The Twilight of the Idols.
Ornstein - Your Two Brains.
Spare - The Book of Pleasure (and others).
Spencer Brown - The Laws of Form.
Steiner - Supplementary Course (and others).
Vaughan - Anthroposophia Theomagica.
Watson - Supernature.

Force and form - twin pillars of the universe, known to us as change and stability, excitement and security or, when malignant, as disruption and stagnation - the demons Lucifer and Ahriman. For too long men have lived under the delusion that this, as with other less fundamental dualities, one should aspire to an ideal point of equilibrium, or 'Christ' state, between the two demonic extremes. But if such a state existed progress towards it would be change and therefore Luciferic, existence in it would be stable and therefore Ahrimanic. Johnstone argued that there could only be a dynamic equilibrium - Christ as the 'Lord of the Dance' - and concluded in his epitaph that 'the only true happiness is to live dangerously in times of peace, and to be at peace in times of crisis'.

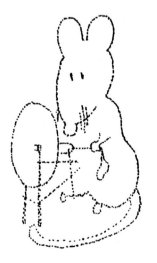

the mouse that spins

MORE FROM THE MOUSEHOLE

If you enjoyed Thundersqueak - or if you did not - you may be intrigued to know about other titles from the same author (under various pseudonyms). Available as e-books from www.occultebooks.com at £3 in screen or printer friendly editions. Some are also available as hard copy .

SSOTBME
REVISED
an essay on magic

Hard copy edition: ISBN 0-904311-08-2 at £12.30

"The book that put the magic back in magic" Gerald Suster

"Quite simply the best introduction to magic I've ever read." Phil Hine, author 'Condensed Chaos', 'Prime Chaos' etc

"Read it, several times. Give it as gifts to those who most NEED to read it. Spread the word, and treasure a universe in which this book exists." Dave Evans www.occultebooks.com

"The global release of this e-edition means that all sentient life on earth now falls into one of two categories, the pre-Ramsey neanderthals and the post-Ramsay illuminati." Pete Carroll, author 'Psychonaut', 'Liber Null', 'The Psychonomicon' etc

"A classic" Li Grainer in Gnosis

"Hooray! It's back at last - SSOTBME, probably the best-ever book on magical theory." Tom Graves, author 'Needles of Stone", "The Dowser's Handbook", "Positively Wyrd" etc

"This book made me realize I was a magician, not insane. Or at least both a magician, and insane. Great, funny, a Grimoire disguised as an essay, only 96 pages long (I like short books, and often, short women), as well as the best book to give to people if you want them to think you are smart and goofy, as opposed to stupid and psychotic. Find it. Buy it. Read it blind drunk the first time, maybe the second time too..."
'Fireclown's basic booklist' from the Internet.

SSOTBME - AN ESSAY ON MAGIC
is now
REVISED!

First published in 1974, SSOTBME immediately established itself as a seminal text of the magical revival. A thinking person's guide to the unthinkable that ran to a second UK edition, a German edition, two Polish editions and a US edition with an Austin Osman Spare print of "The Blase Bacchante" on the cover.

The book became an essential text for the Chaos Magic current, which it partly inspired. At the other end of the magical spectrum, it was a significant influence upon the later New Age movement through its clear exposition of the extent to which our world is shaped by our beliefs.

Long since out of print, SSOTBME is now available as a paperback or e-book. What's more, it has been brought right up to date and enlarged with additional commentary to over 150 pages by Ramsey Dukes (sorry about that, Fireclown!).

The difference, and the relationship, between science, art, religion and magic. The nature of magical theory - with examples from alchemy, astrology, ritual magic, Feng Shui, tarot reading and other systems of divination. A discussion of the role of sacrifice, of demons, of cyber-animism and initiation. A concise and comprehensive survey of every aspect of modern magic and its place in our world.

It's a new, definitive magical grimoire for the 21st century, and it's available now from Web-orama or bookshops.

THE NAKED, SHOCKING TRUTH BEHIND THE INTER-NATIONAL SATANIC CONSPIRACY

No question was more hotly debated by the International Satanic Executivein the mid 70s than this: should they come out into the open, or should they continue to corrupt civilisation discreetly from behind the scenes?

No voice will be better remembered than that of the Honourable Hugo CStJ l'Estrange, Minister for Moral Decline and grand old man of British Satanism, arguing that the election of Margaret Thatcher was a clear signalthat his country was weary of 60s idealism and was crying out for True Evil to lead the way forward.

Because of this stirring appeal, Satanism went public - with Hugol'Estrange's "Satanists Diary" appearing as a regular column in Aquarian Arrow. No-one could deny the ensuing moral and spiritual decline throughout our society consequent upon this exercise.

In this volume we present the entire unexpurgated Satanist's Diary in all its evil glory. Here you can meet such vile personages as: Dr Sigismund Galganspiel, Minister for Absolute Evil; Miss Florence Dashwood, of the Cheltenham Ladies' Lilith Association; the Very Irreverend Dr Eival B Myeghud DSat, DipDiab, MDem Bishop of the Church of Eternal Damnation; Dr Wunlita Suzuki, Bodhisattva of the Nez School; Ernest Synner, Student Representative... and others too revolting for words.

THE HELLGATE CHRONICLES
FIFTEEN YEARS OF SIN AND CORRUPTION
available as e-book from www.occultebooks.com.

A hard copy version will become available once we've sold sufficient drugs, guns, prostitutes and share options to finance the publication.

Words
Made
Flesh

Virtual reality, humanity & the cosmos

New edition: ISBN 0-904311-11-2. £14

The book that first proposed and explored in depth the idea
that we might be living in virtual reality - that information
could be more fundamental than either matter or energy -
more than a decade before the idea was popularised in films
like Open Your Eyes and The Matrix.

For some the greatest significance of this model is that it
transforms our expectations of the universe from material to
magical models. It is no longer ridiculous to see connections
between the positions of the stars, the play of tarot cards or
yarrow stalks and everyday life - for independent, random
phenomena are extremely costly in terms of information and
would have been most unlikely to have evolved in the virtual
universe's struggle for processing resources.

It has taken more than a dozen years for the ideas in this
book to be given serious consideration in New Scientist and
other popular science media - meanwhile the author has
forged ahead with further essays and explorations of the
theme which have been appended to this new second edition.

**Available as hard copy from bookshops and as e-book and
hard copy from www.occultebooks.com**

BLAST

your way to megabuck$
with my *SECRET*
sex-power formula...
and other reflections upon the spiritual path

Volume Two
of the collected essays of Ramsey Dukes

Available as e-book from www.occultebooks.com

He appears more than ever a combination of Robert Anton Wilson and
Tommy Cooper... The Peter Pan of the British occult scene, and long
may he go on diverting us.
Paul Geheimnis, Chaos International No 15

For an unbeatable title see 'Blast Your Way to Megabuck$ With My
SECRET Sex Power Formula' - thoughts on masculism, magic and the
metaworld from Ramsey Dukes. Virtual Gonzo.
David Profumo, Daily Telegraph Books Of The Year, November '93

Something of Arthur Koestler, something of Loa Tzu, a pinch of Kant
and a dash of Genghis Kahn - Ramsay Dukes is magnificent...
Humourous, witty, written with flair and economy of style, this is certainly one of the most thought provoking and genuinely radical books
I've read in a long while. If you are hacked off with old ideas and yearn
for new vistas, you could do a lot worse than let Ramsey Dukes be
your guide.
Julian Vayne, Pagan Voice Autumn '93

☞Why does there seem to be less magic in the modern world? *Could it be because we are all better magicians?*

☞Is it time to reinstate the Charlatan in his vital role as initiator on the occult path?

☞Is scientific thought declining in favour of magical thought, and is this inevitable?

☞Have men traditionally played a leading roles because of a deep sense of their own uselessness relative to women? *And is this situation beginning to reverse?*

☞Might we not be living with another's virtual reality? *How would this effect our understanding of this universe?*

These and other questions are explored in depth in this volume that brings together essays written in the 1980s by one of the most original and creative contemporary writers on magic.

Open your mind to a breath of fresh air
from Ramsey Dukes

What I did in my holidays
Essays on Black Magic, Satanism, Devil Worship and other niceties

Volume Three
of the collected essays of Ramsey Dukes

Is it ok for a national government to negotiate with terrorists?

Should we be prepared to make a pact with the demon Terrorism - or should we remain forever sworn to the demon No Compromise?

This is a book about demonolatry.

It was never meant to be: it began as a cobbling together of all the essays and stuff written in the last seven years. But it turned out to have a pretty consistent theme.

A theme that begins with Crowley's "Aeon of Horus" and the new, Thelemic morality. From that viewpoint demonic pacts are re-appraised: are they not a negotiation with the demonic, as opposed to sworn allegiance?

Many old and new demons lurk on these pages: black magic, sexism, elitism, satanism, publishers, prejudice, suicide, liberalism, violence, slime, bitterness, old age, war and the New Age.

These demons hold keys to power and wisdom.

They are prepared to negotiate.

Are you?

ISBN 1-869928-520
First edition, 1998, published in collaboration with The Mouse That Spins (TMTS) by: Mandrake of Oxford.
410pp Felstead 80gsm paper, stitch bound.
Now available from any bookshop at £18
Or from Mandrake of Oxford, PO Box 250, Oxford OX1 1AP. UK
or from www.occultebooks.com

Printed in the United Kingdom
by Lightning Source UK Ltd.
9446700001B